# ENDORSEMENTS

Greg Clary knows—and loves—his place. He loves it so much he wants to make us love it, too. And—as this book demonstrates in poem after poem, he does. Clary wears his heart on his sleeve, and puts it smack on the page.

All of Clary's senses are alive, and he has the language to infuse them with his deep observation. Clary's sensitive vision profoundly understands the miracle in each moment, the hero in each soul. He's a poet of passion and compassion. His photographic eye notices the bearded man sitting yoga under the Dollar General sign and his tuned hear can distinguish the conversations in the checkout line. It's a relief to encounter a poet that speaks in his own accent, chronicle the gestures in the hospital waiting room, in the corner bar.

Clary is the Whitman of West Virginia, honoring the laborers, the precious encounters, the deeper wisdoms. He understands intimately that life itself is poetry. Read this book and understand why we need to live it, why we need write it, why we need to read it, and the hopeful lessons we gain by it:

"I learned that/things work out in the end./And if they don't,/it's not the end."

And, unlike life, when we get to this book's end, we just go back to the beginning and read it all again.

Philip Terman, author of:
*My Blossoming Everything*
*This Crazy Devotion*

# THE
# VANDALIA
# IN
# ME

A PHOTO-POETRY COLLECTION FROM APPALACHIA

# THE VANDALIA IN ME

GREG CLARY

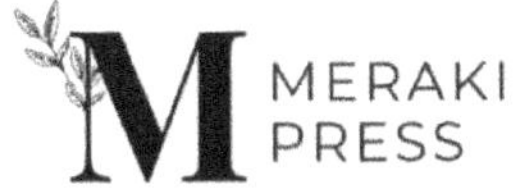

MERAKI PRESS

To my beloved Cassie Mae,
whose love and support made
every page possible.

# TABLE OF CONTENTS

*photographs and poems share a title*


13 *Acknowledgments*
14 *Head On into the Dirt:*
   *An Introduction on Greg Clary*
17 Vandalia in Me
21 In the Crook of a Tree Along the
   Clarion River
23 Chalk Eye
25 Radio Preacher
27 New York City, August 7, 1974
29 Going Home
31 The Bowery, 1975
33 Overheard
35 Redemption
37 Sugar
39 Places I Slept During My
   Misspent Youth
41 Eaglet Dreams
42 Unrepentant
44 Deer Hunt Haiku
45 Iron Horse
46 Mabel
49 Kansas City Star
51 (One) Last Time
53 Introvert Hell
55 Thinking Outside the Bar
57 After Dark, Before Dawn
59 Drinking With Jerry Jeff
61 She Wrote Maya Angelou
62 Playground Ghosts
63 Time to Sing
65 Tell Me a Story
67 Impresarios of Memory
69 Iron City Christmas
71 Charm
72 Deer Season

73 Down at Rachael's
75 1959
77 Fourth of July on the Clarion River
79 Black Coffee
81 While Waiting to Change Worlds
83 Check-out Line
85 Iron Mike
87 Lessons From My 3rd Grade Teacher
89 Existential Angst of a 5-Year-Old
91 Soaps and Ice
93 He Won't Ever Be Gone
95 Learning to wait
97 Uncle Wilmer: A Debt to the Devil
99 Texting With My College Roommate
   After 40 Years
103 Online Dating
105 Conundrum
107 Saying Hello to an Old Goodbye
109 How to Host a Good Party
111 A Good Day
113 37 Things I Like
115 Skills
117 Time of the Varse
119 Fortuity
121 24 Hours
123 Today Was a Good Day
125 Back to the Steel City Lounge
127 Who is Virgil Tate?
129 Black Friday
131 Remembrance
133 Lunch at the Korner Restaurant
137 Where Do You Think You Are----1957?
139 *About the Author*

# ACKNOWLEDGMENTS

Grateful acknowledgement is made to the editors of these publications
where several of the photographs
and poems appeared:'

*Anti-Heroin Chic*
*Appalachian Lit*
*Black Shamrock Magazine*
*Change Seven*
*Clinch*
*Detour Ahead*
*Fourth River*
*Hole in the Head Review*
*Looking at Appalachia*
*Northern Appalachia Review*
*North/South Appalachia*
*Off the Coast Magazine*
*Pine Mountain Sand & Gravel*
*Pittsburgh Post-Gazette*
*Rattle*
*Rust Belt*
*Rusty Truck*
*Sterling Clack Clack*
*The Bridge Literary Journal*
*The Watershed Journal*
*Tiny Seed Journal*
*Tobeco*
*Trailer Park Quarterly*
*Wingless Dreamer*
*Wild Wind*

# HEAD ON INTO THE DIRT:
# AN INTRODUCTION TO GREG CLARY

I was going to crack a joke to start this introduction, to say what a bargain you're holding, a great collection of poems and a great collection of photographs, all bundled together for the price of an upscale six pack. But this book is something special, and it delivers plenty of laughs on its own, funny lines mixed with a fierce beauty and the great hardships so many people are experiencing around the country.

The Vandalia Greg Clary creates is as real as Raymond Carver's *Pacific Northwest* or Flannery O'Connor's *South*. It's a wild place filled with love and dreams. His world is an Appalachia Ann Pancake would love, one filled with deer hunting, rivers, and family. Biscuits and fried green tomatoes. It is hospital visits and rough bars and demolition derby. But it's also
Mike Tyson dropping in for some common-sense dialogue and Amish folks with cheap reels fishing on the river. It's a young person from West Virginia stumbling around New York City, looking to take the best things home. The unexpected in this collection makes the expected all the more exciting. I love hearing about Jerry Jeff Walker—outlaw and songwriting hero—drunk after a show, giving advice. I love all the dying friends and relatives believing we'll meet up in Heaven.

I doubt many poets could link up Hank Williams, Henry David Thoreau, and a generous pool hustler named Chalk Eye, but they're all here, working for a better world. The music is endless: Del McCoury, Stonewall Jackson, the Jerry Garcia Band.

It's easy to find bad things in the world. Hunter Thompson, when the drinking and drugs had taken his talent, mostly sounded like a complainer. Lester Bangs built a career out of humiliating musicians. Step into the internet and someone will tell you we're all ruined.

Greg Clary's art rejects the simple notions of doom. I don't mean to say that these poems and photographs turn away from the messiness of the world. The bad is here. You can end up in a jail cell for a couple drinks. You can get punched for almost nothing. Buildings fall apart and rot.

But the good news and the bad news sit side by side in this book.

Here are the radio preachers condemning us all. Here are the lost dreams of Richard Brautigan and the hippies. I don't want to give away too much, but this line,

"Someday Love will die, and Time will bury it," is one of the saddest I've ever read.

Then you find a poem capturing the spirit of an elementary school teacher.

Then you see a photograph of the most beautiful dive bar ever.

The hope here is bountiful.

I've never seen poor and working-class folks and the places they go to save themselves photographed with such honesty. The shots of even the most rundown bars are filled with the brightness of dreams and possibility. I've never seen anyone photograph an American flag—whether on boots or hanging in a window—with more meaning and compassion. The

characters in these pages fall because that's what people do. But after the headline, after the mistake—that's what Greg Clary does so well. This is how we're all still loved. This is how we all have a chance, even after chance. His poem about Johnny Paycheck is as good as Bukowski's poem about Borodin. His poem about hitchhiking to Florida is Jack Kerouac dunked in the spirit of West Virginia.

The dialogue in these poems crackles with realism, the kind of language that sounds perfect in a John Sayles film or in a documentary about Harlan County. The characters look and sound like Hemingway if Hemingway had grown up in a holler.

If I were writing a blurb for this book, or if I were just recommending it to a friend, I'd use this word: dignity. It's an idea completely lost in popular American culture, but here's a guy from a tiny town in West Virginia, who ended up a professor, who is old enough to be dead but still loves to hunt and fish, who—through some miracle—found a pen and a camera after he

retired and captured a small world with the widest possible lens.

Thank god for art and those who make it.

Thank god for Greg Clary.

I hope you enjoy this book as much as I did.

--Dave Newman, author of
*She Throws Herself Forward to Stop the Fall*
*East Pittsburgh Down Low*

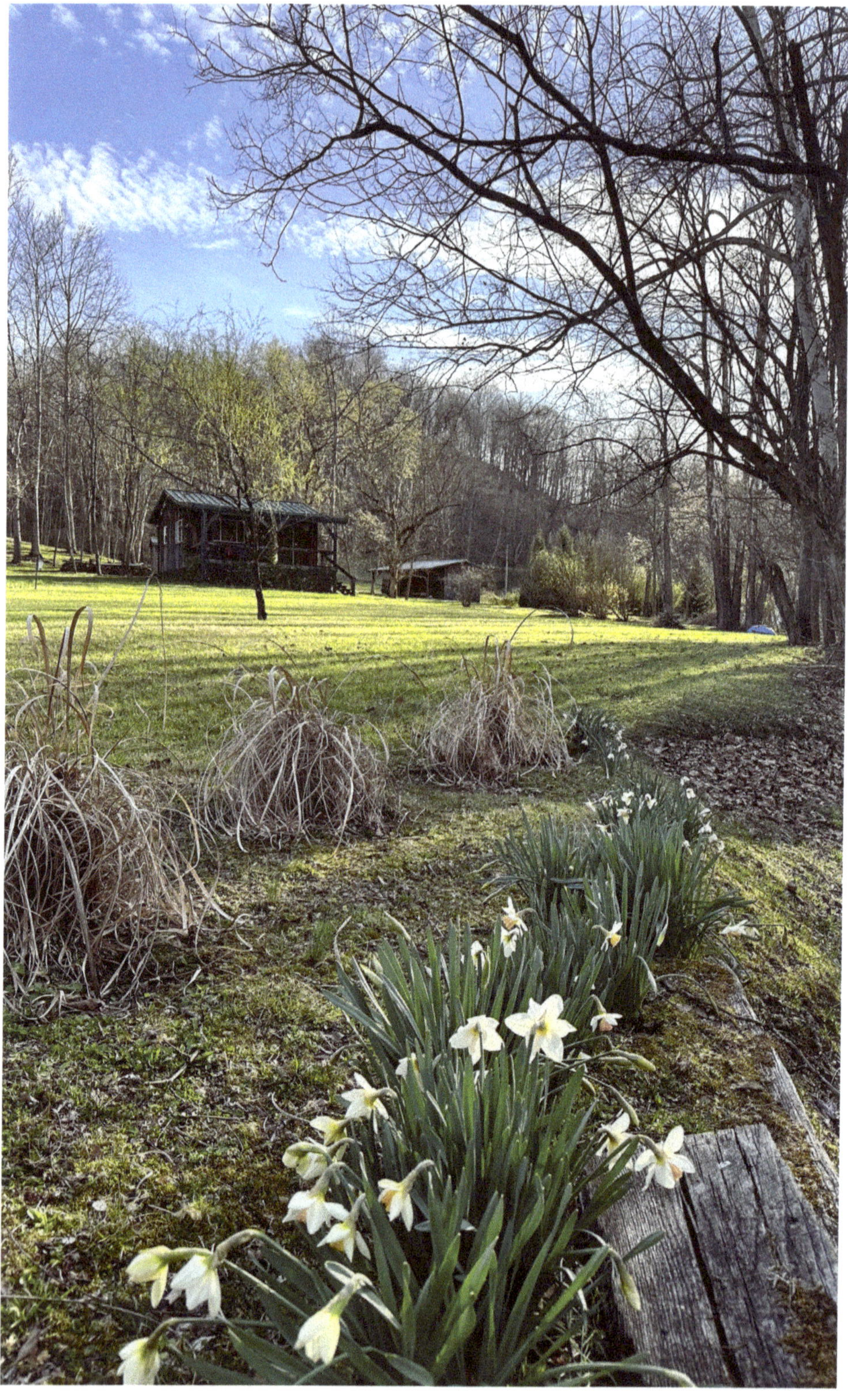

Vandalia in Me

Bring out
the ginseng in me.
The freckled red-head gigging frogs
growing up
in splendid isolation,
pintos and cornbread
every day.

Bring out
the double-murder ballads,
the Buckeye pot belly stove,
the Breece and Ann Pancake,
the washed in the blood Holy Ghost,
the burley tobacco's green-horn worms,
the Camels, Falls City, and scratch-off.
The belief in the mercy of the world.
The Mothman in me.

Bring out
the coal tattoo in me.
The homely holler hoopie
watching his Papaw
enter the cage and descend
with wordless grit
every day.

Bring out
the Celtic Cross in me,
the wariness of exploitation,
the deep rooted cynicism,
the despair of outlander colonization,
the despisal of Ulster Plantation repression,
the contempt for disrespect.

Bring out
the fiery temper
at insolent pity,
the hard Hazel Dickens fatalism of life
to be endured.
The Hallelujah
anyway.

I am
musk melon, pawpaws, rhubarb pie,
slaw dogs, ramps.
Saturday night bluegrass,
Sunday morning stained glass,
a lonesome whip-poor-will
at twilight, yearning to sing.

I will always get back up,
with gratitude for the
enduring grip of grace
this day.
And every day after.

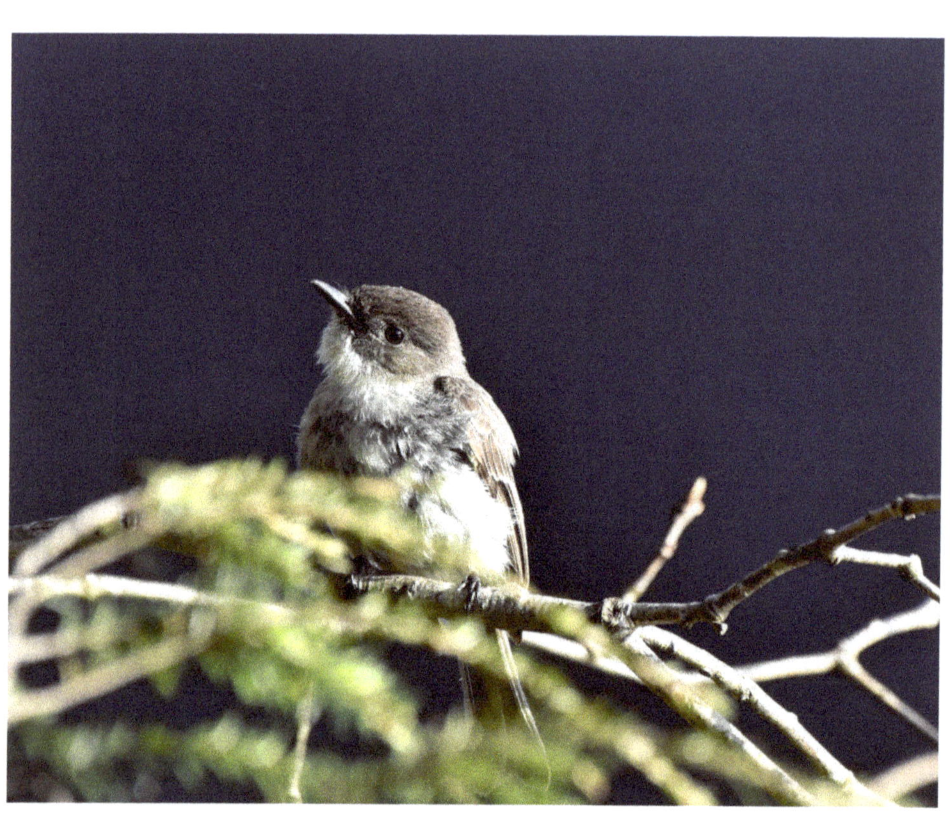

In the Crook of a Tree Along the Clarion River

Below my conifer-spray perch
on the bank of the river,
kayakers quietly slide by
with rhythmic strokes,
passing a jon-boat of
Zebco-casting Amish fishermen and
a pontoon boat of wet,
Bud Light sipping pensioners,
soaked by the spray of
their grandkids on roaring jet skis.

Do they notice
the river's jade tint, or
the steep pitch of
hemlocks, pines, and oaks
towering above on both sides,
shapeshifting the water below
into mirrored trees?

Do they hear
the scolding trill of a
Phoebe, agitated by a
fat water snake sunning
on a warm boulder?

A momentary scene,
an enduring memory.
Wondering what
became of Phoebe?

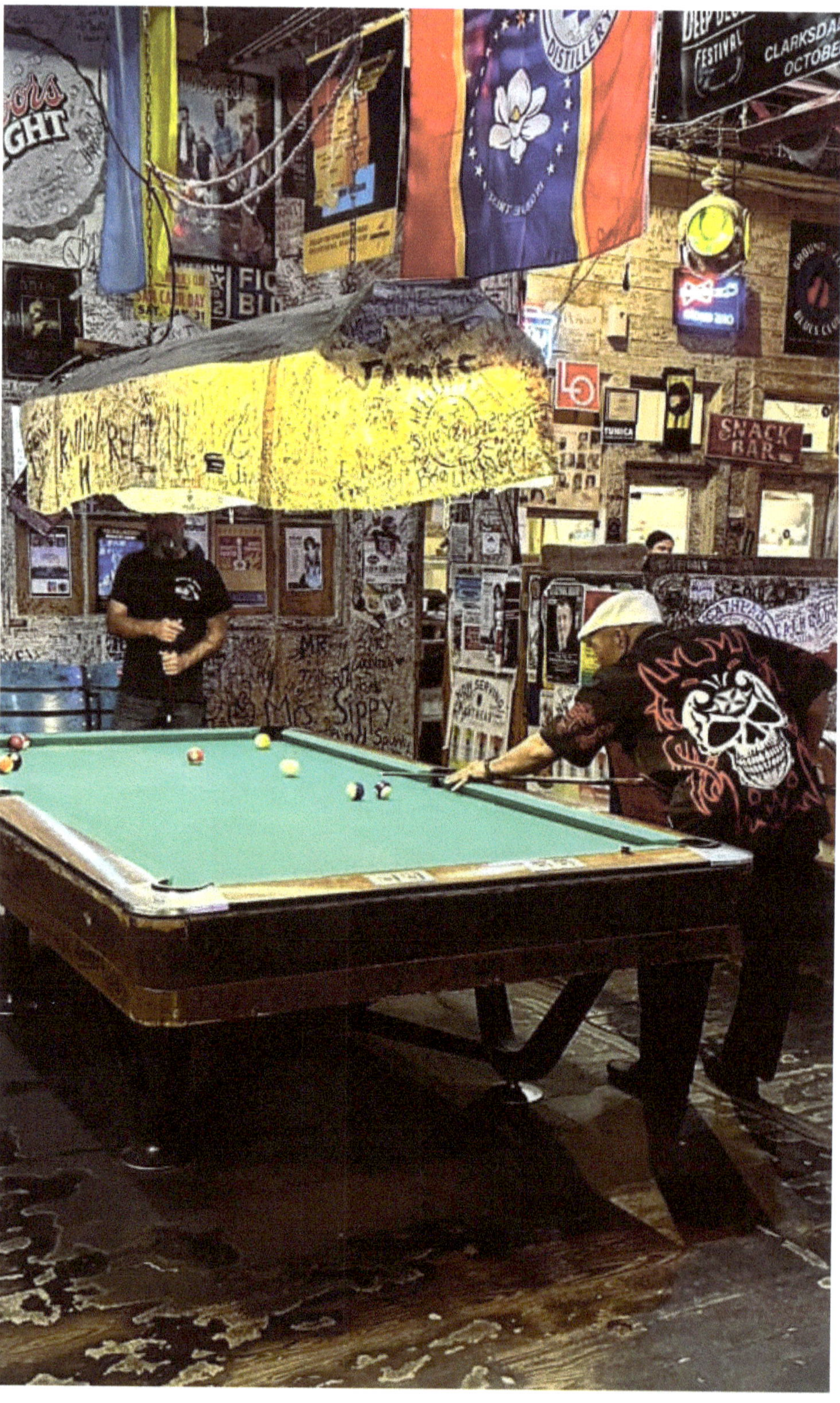

Chalk Eye

Thoreau lived uncelebrated
and nearly broke.
Genius is often disguised when it walks among us.
It often dies unnoticed, like Hank Williams,
in the back of a 1952 Cadillac.

My old honcho, Chalk Eye,
cobalt blue eyes, long steely fingers,
made his living hustling
in juke joint pool halls.

He took me in saying,
"Kid, your next shot should
set up your next shot.
Never mistake bad play for bad luck.
Take a hangover to being served bad ice."

Chalk Eye laughed, mostly at himself.
He drank too much.
He'd take your last dollar bet, then
give it back to you if he thought you needed it.
Like Thoreau, Chalk Eye preferred truth over money

That kind of pool player is rare.
That type of person is rarer.
Chalk Eye gave me Hank Williams.
Both were the rarest of all.

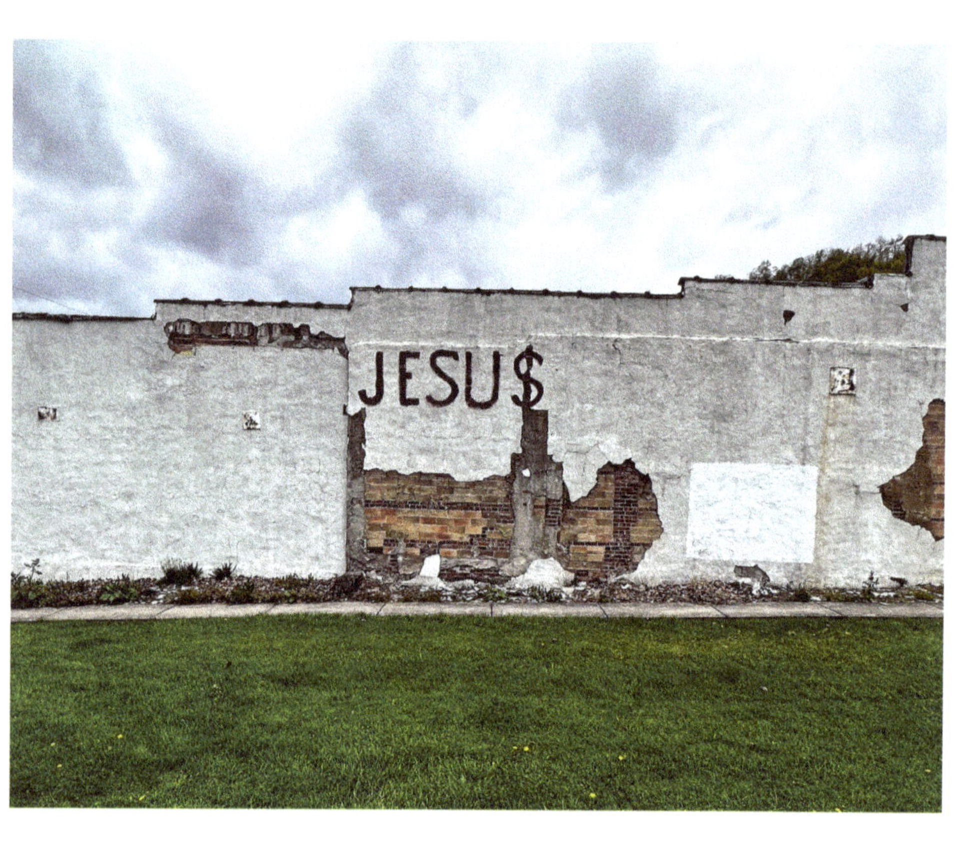
JESU$

Radio Preacher

The Radio Preacher has had it
 with heathens, unbelievers, and idolaters
who worship affluence and worldliness.

He is galled with prosperity sermonizers
who claim that believers may
 obtain riches from God,
 simply by writing out a check.

> *I don't care if you've been dunked in*
> *every creek in the county, so*
> *the minners know you by name,*
> *unless you're saved and washed in the blood*
> *you are lost forever.*

> *I've had it with unclean spirts and*
> *educated fools who obey Satan:*
> *movie stars, athletes, celebrities, college professors.*
> *Most are in hell or heading there soon.*

College professors?
A little close to home.

He has more:
> *Sometimes I'm asked to write a letter*
> *of reference for college and I'll say*
> *what good Christians these students are.*

> *I always close with:*
> *I hope this child doesn't get some*
> *God-hating, infidel professor, who will*
> *drag'em down to hell with'em.*

Here it comes.
Surely, this time
Radio Preacher will call out my name
right through the airwaves.
But he fades off
like a forecasted storm
that never comes.

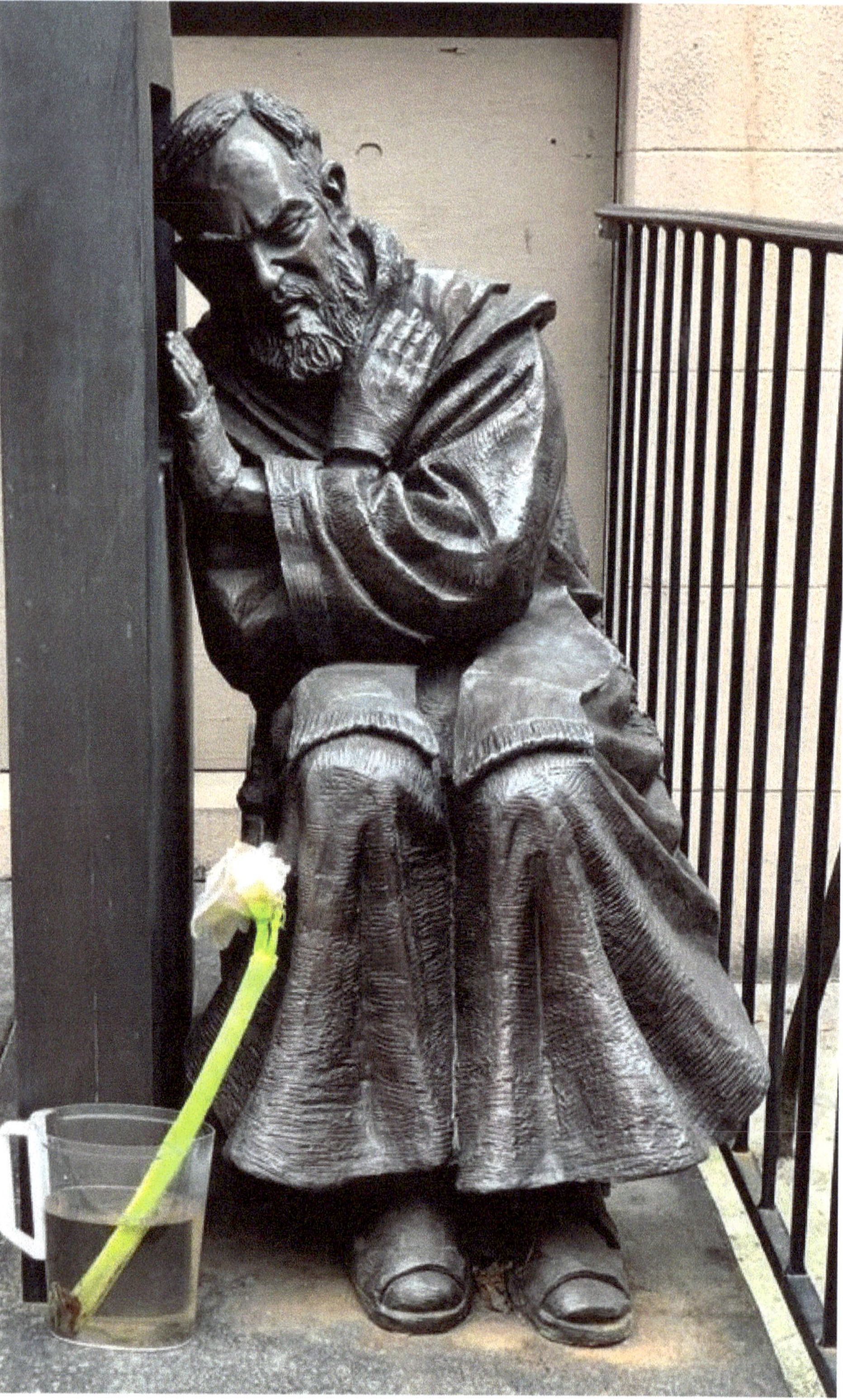

New York City, August 7, 1974

We were new at this grown-up stuff.
Me reading your beat poets and
you listening to my Gram Parsons
in the faint light of a dripping candle
stuck into a Mateus Rose' bottle.

Dawn brought this headline:
"Nixon Resigns!"
And the view of a daring Frenchman
walking a tightrope between the Twin Towers.

We stare out your Battery Park
pocket window as Gram sang:
*"So if you want a do right all day woman,
you gotta be a do right all night man."*

We descended into each other
while you whispered Brautigan:
"Someday Time will die, and Love will bury it."

We believed it.
We thought that's how it would go.
But, no. We had it backwards:
*"Someday Love will die, and Time will bury it."*

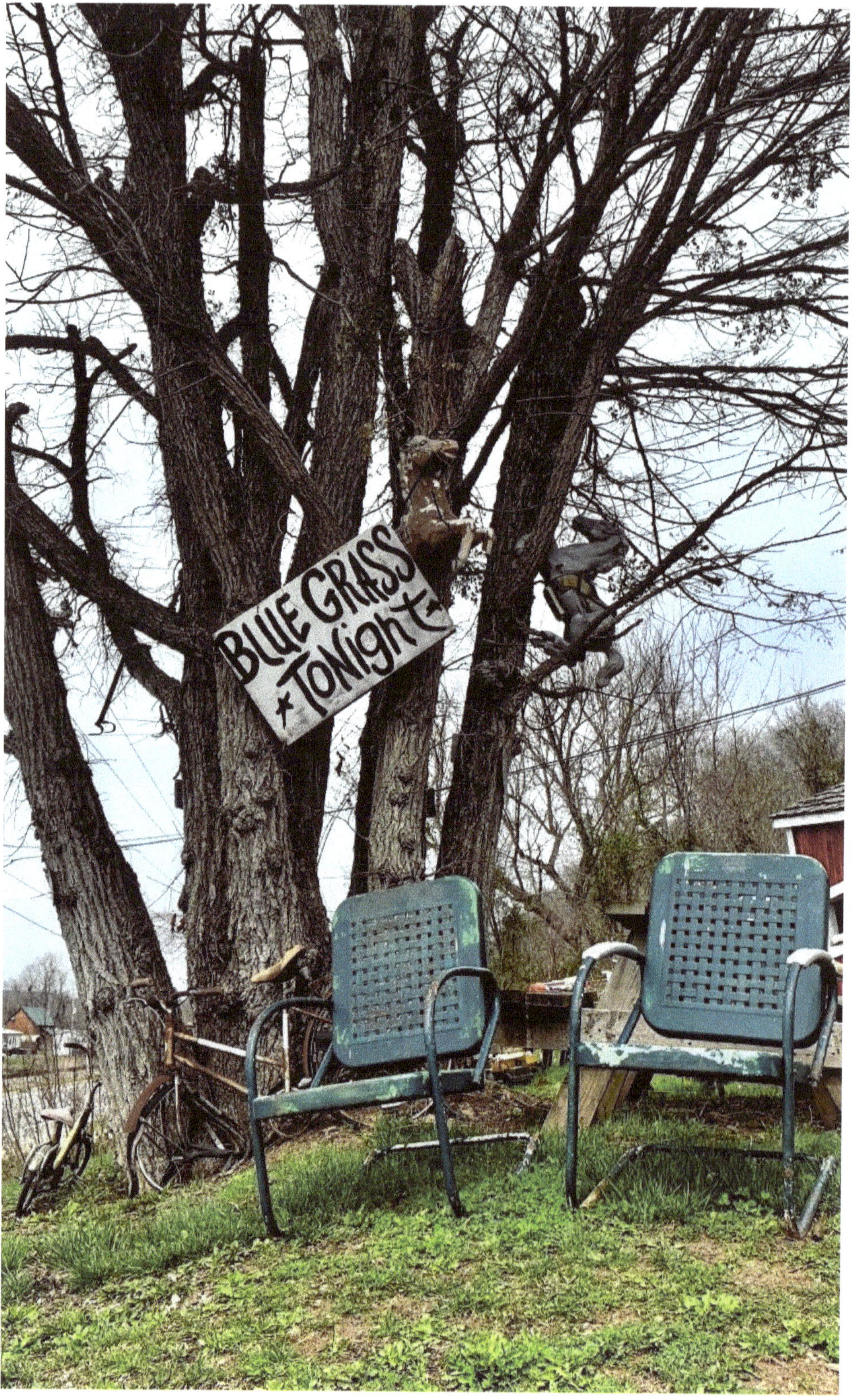
BLUE GRASS
TONight

Going Home

Last week, I listened to
a Syrian poet from Damascus
share how homesick he was
for a place where he loved everyone
and everyone loved him.

Afterwards, I told him how his
words gripped me.
How it reminded me of a song:
*I lived in the mountains*
*I had a lot of fun*
*I knew a lot of people and*
*I loved everyone around me.*

Damascus, Syria, became
Turkey Creek, West Virginia.

This morning, I drink coffee
at the cabin,
thinking of good friends,
some no longer around,
who sat in this kitchen,
eating, drinking, laughing,
being imperfect.

My great-aunt Frankie used to say:
*Moments never stay, but*
*memories do.*

She used to say all those things.

I realize
I am being nostalgic for
a time that really isn't over.
I listen to my son's bluegrass CD.
Read a friend's book of poetry.
Look at pictures of gatherings gone by.
And respond to a text that pings:

*Hey, Clary, how long*
*you going to be in?*
*We need to get together.*

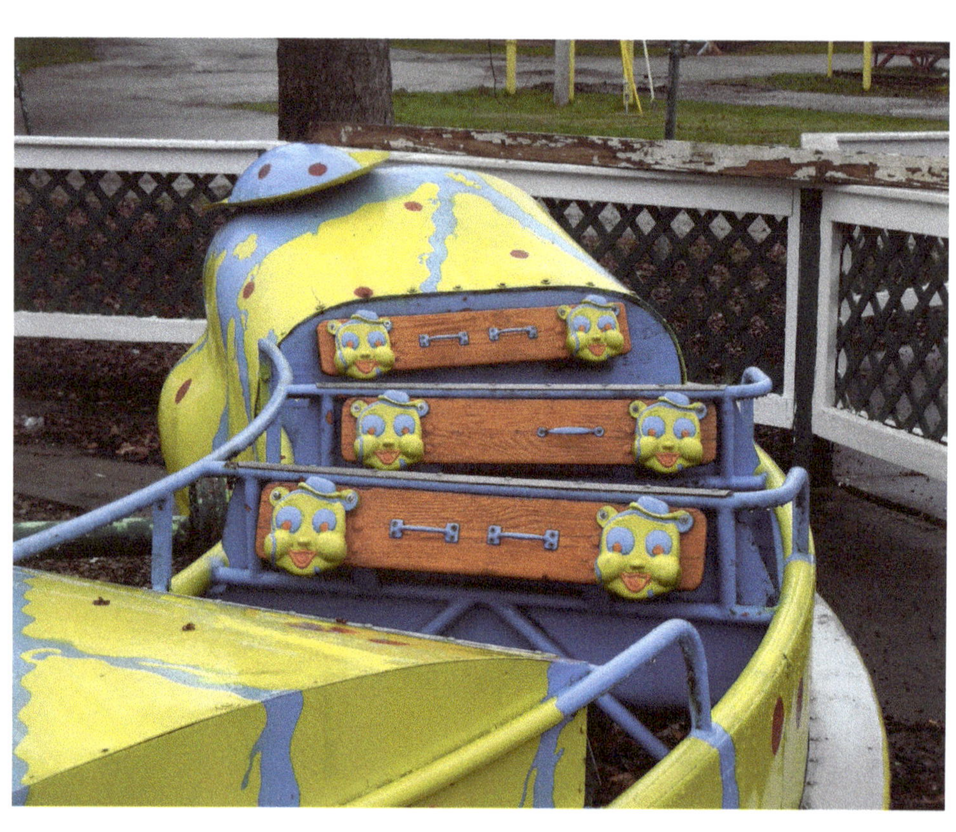

Wet tables,
sticky floor,
quarter drafts,
cover band
playing nonstop.
A rowdy gong on
the cowbell
hanging from
the ceiling
after a big tip.
And if it's
big enough,
Sugar Bear will
hop on
stage and sing
Mustang Sally
while flashing her
kitchen table tattoo,
Can't Touch This

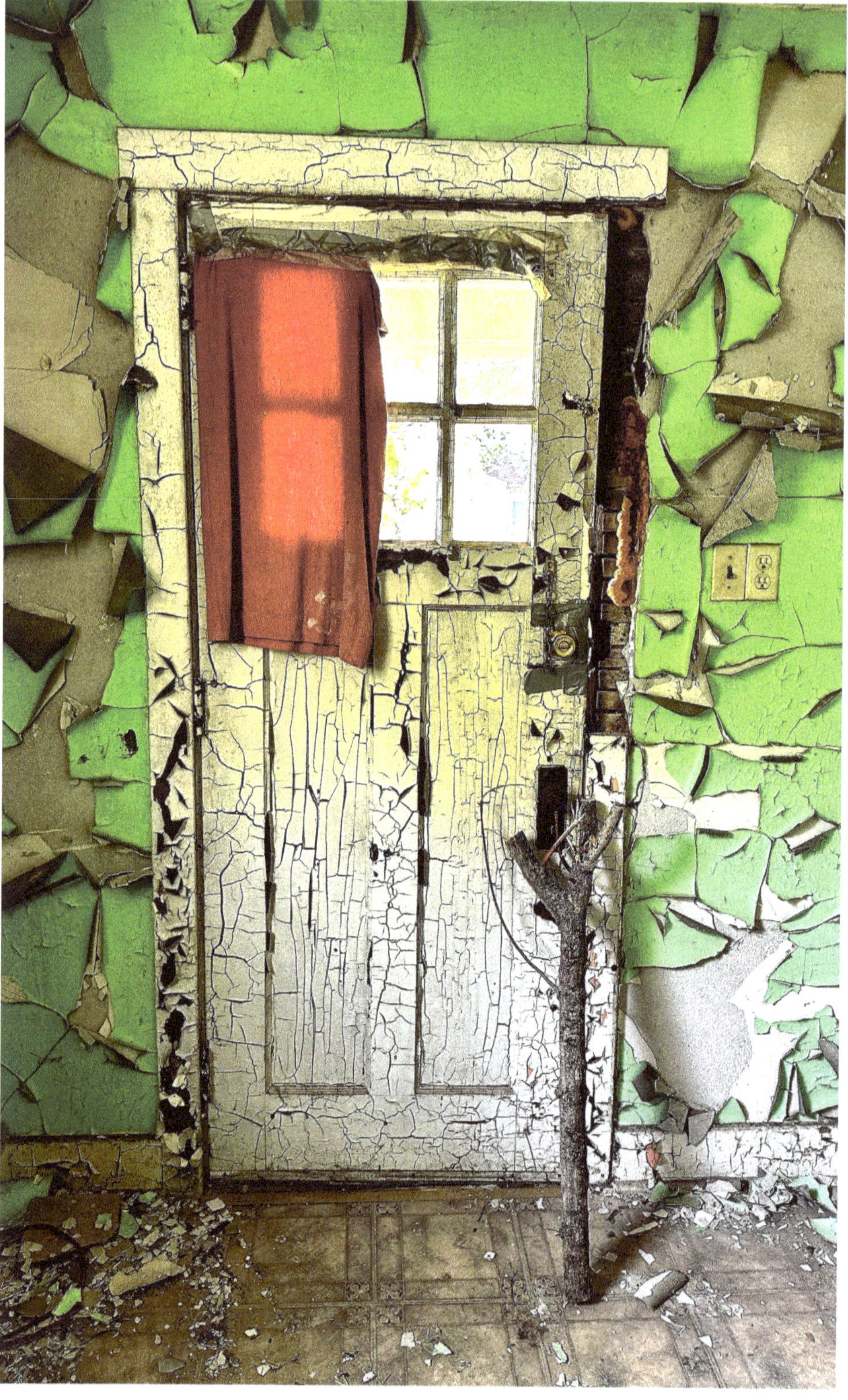

Overheard

Making a Dollar Store run
for the necessities:
milk, eggs, beer, scratch-off.
Listening to small talk
in the check-out line:


A ribby looking woman murmured,
*I wished they carried fresh vegetables here.*
The guy with her laughed, *What for?*
*You don't eat vegetables.*
She paused, *Well, tobacco. I get about 50 servings a day.*


Older fella in JC Penney cover-alls:
*We once had a beagle dog that was*
*good on rabbits. Never had a name.*
*We just called it Roger's Dog.*


Two 40ish women in conversation:
*I'd rather commit adultery than have this root canal*


2nd woman: *Well, who wouldn't?*


Skinny dude in a Red Rose feed cap:
*A shotgun is all you need for your home.*
*Don't have to worry about a slug going through a wall.*
*I keep mine behind the couch for the wife to use.*


*Just let her deal with it*


An elderly woman talking to
a young mother holding her baby,
*Well, I wish good luck to the little feller*
*'cause he's come into a hard world.*

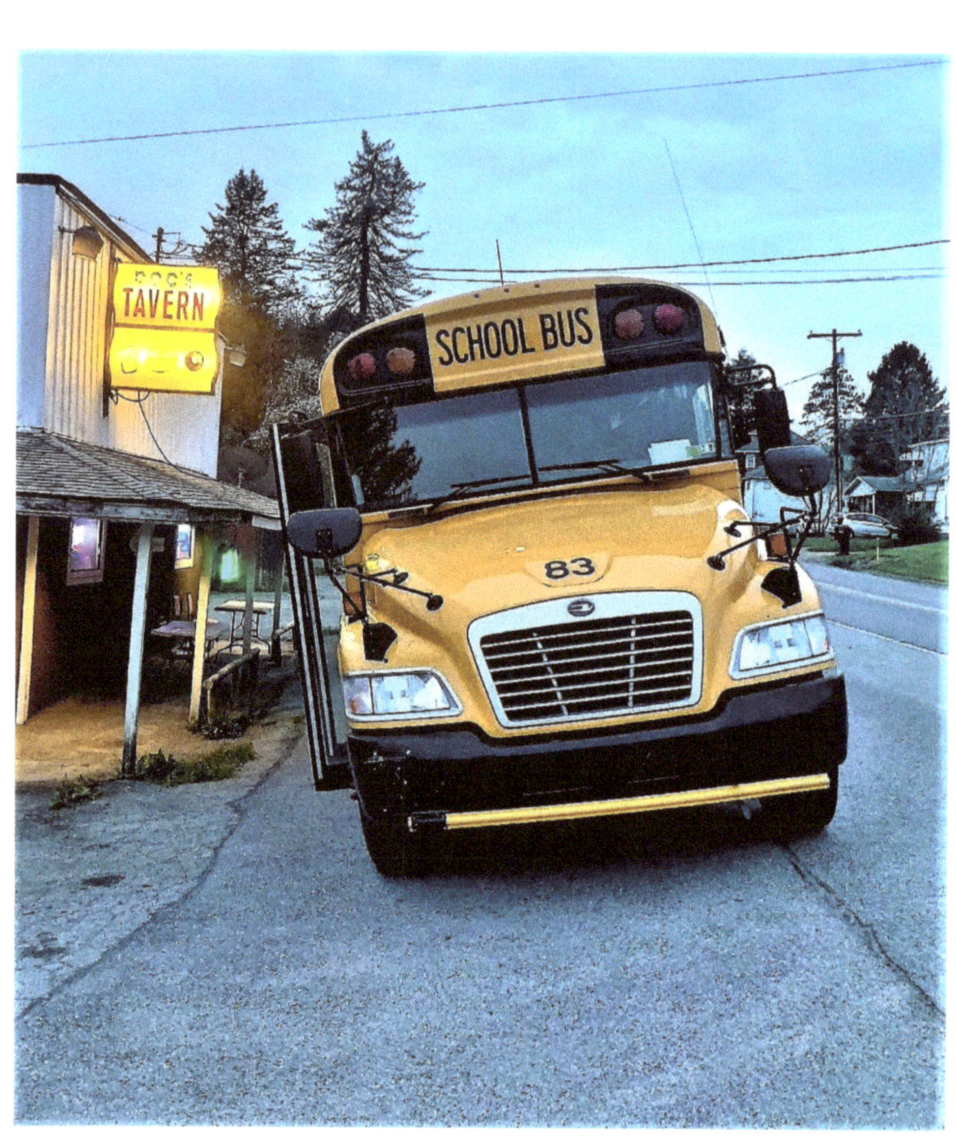

TAVERN
SCHOOL BUS
83

Redemption

Sundays nights at The Lantern
meant hunch dancing around
the shuffleboard table to
a country band playing
*Wasted Days and Wasted Nights.*

That's where she found me.
 At the bar nursing
a tall Falls City,
shrouded in blue smoke,
 measuring one more
Ghost of Regret.

She was heading
 home to Pittsburgh
to patch things up with her fiancé.
A great guy.
She never lied or misled me.
Her future always meant him.
But we did have us some fun
before saying what we thought
needed to be said.

As the band shifted into
Merle's *Swinging Doors,*
 a familiar arm
 hugged my neck from behind.
*"You have got to get out of here,"* she whispered

*"Let me finish my beer first,"* I eagerly replied

She swatted my head,
*"No, you knucklehead, not that!*
*Look at me.*
*You have to leave this town.*
*This life you're living.*
*There is more for you.*
*But it's not here."*

She spoke truth.
 I actually listened for once.

Chances were taken.
Cautiously.
Changes were made.
Slowly.
I learned that
things work out in the end.
And if they don't,
it's not the end.

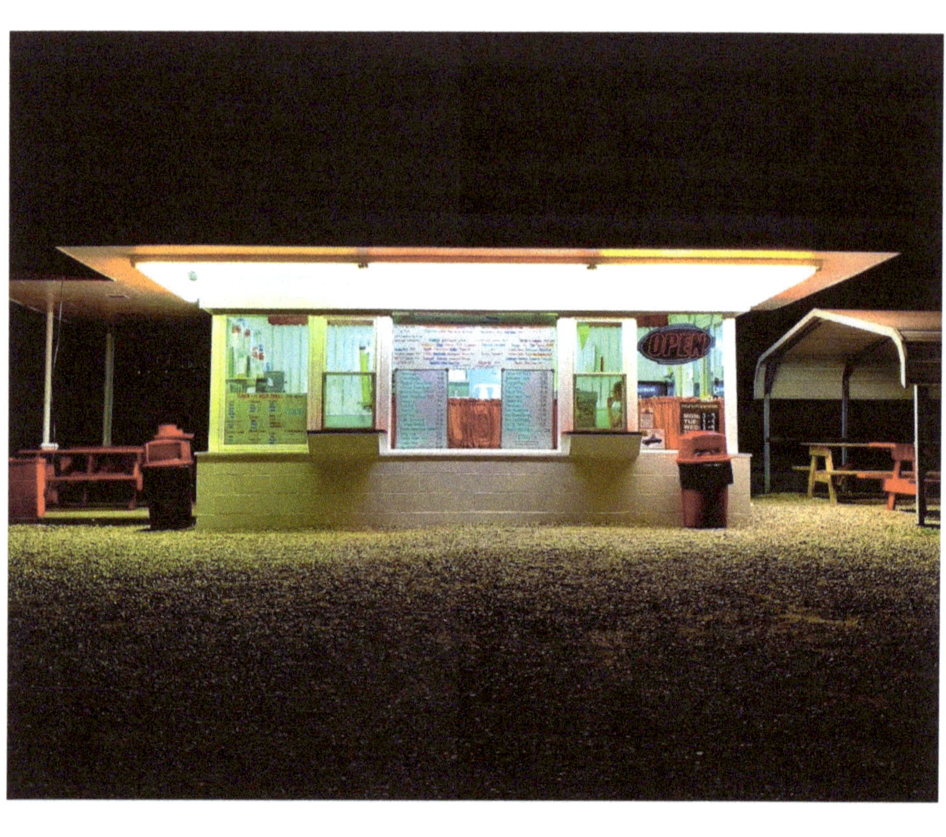

Sugar

Returning home to West Virginia and hearing
*Hey Baby, Darlin, Honey.*
*What can I get you?*
*How you doing?*
From unfamiliar women.
I miss those sweet terms of affection.
But, Sugar is what gets me.
Every time.

Tips are automatically doubled,
unintended purchases are made.
My heart melts.
Every time.

Today, sitting alone in the woods,
I got to thinking.
Sugar. Why sugar?

Then, a vision. An awareness. An image.
My mother died just as I turned 3, and
her oldest sister, my Aunt June,
would stop by, pick me up,
turn me upside down,
rough me up, make me laugh.
And call me Sugar.
Every time.

Something I needed,
but could not name.
Something I still need
when I come home each day.
Every time.

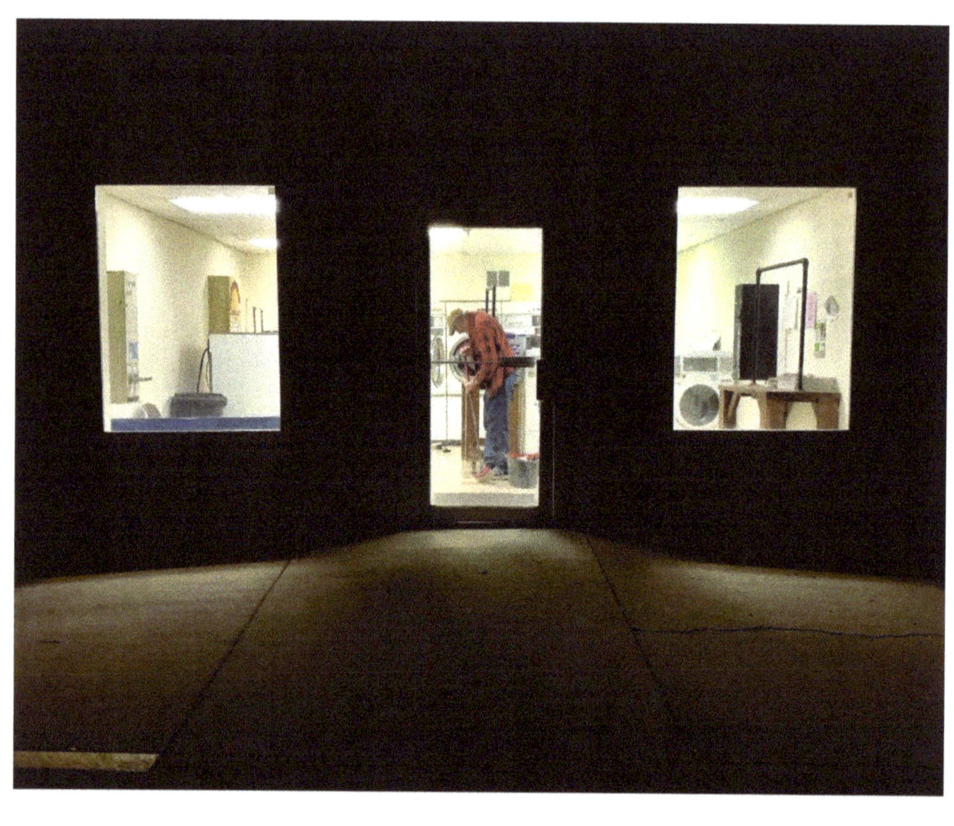

Places I Slept During My Misspent Youth

My cousin's horse barn.
    [They didn't mind because they knew I didn't smoke.]
The backseat of another cousin's 1967 ragtop Pontiac GTO,
    [He kept a wool blanket for reasons I didn't quite understand at the time.]
Under interstate bridges while hitching all around the south.
    [Noisy, secure, and dry.]
In the drunk tank in Huntington, West Virginia after being arrested by a cop with
whom I shared a Sociology class.
    [We never acknowledged each other again.]
On the couch of a Unification Church (Moonies).
    [Dinner was better than the endless catechism that followed.]
In the back of a Greyhound bus traveling from Florida to West Virginia with stops
at every crossroad heading north.
    [I jumped off somewhere in Kentucky and hitched the rest of the way in.]
Under an open-sided pavilion at an RV campground,
    [Before waking up to a crowd of kids on spyder bikes circled around to see if I
     was alive or dead.]
Hidden behind a chaise lounge on the 7th floor swimming pool deck of the Adams
Hotel in Phoenix, Arizona,
    [after missing the last bus back to a friend's college dorm.]
In the Tampa Stockade in Tampa, Florida after being jailed for hitchhiking on Inter-
state-75.
    [The longest night of my life.]
In Mrs. Daniels' 11:00 English class nearly every day of my junior year in high
school.
    [It was not her fault.]
Cheap motel rooms all around Myrtle Beach.
    [The Pink House, not far from the Pavilion, was a favorite at $ 5.00 per night.]
By my grandpa's hospital bed
    [as he lay dying.]
A horse trailer, with a horse,
    [at Camden Amusement Park].
Now, 50 years later, when I stop at a traffic light, I will sometimes look around and
think to myself:
    I could sleep there if I had to.

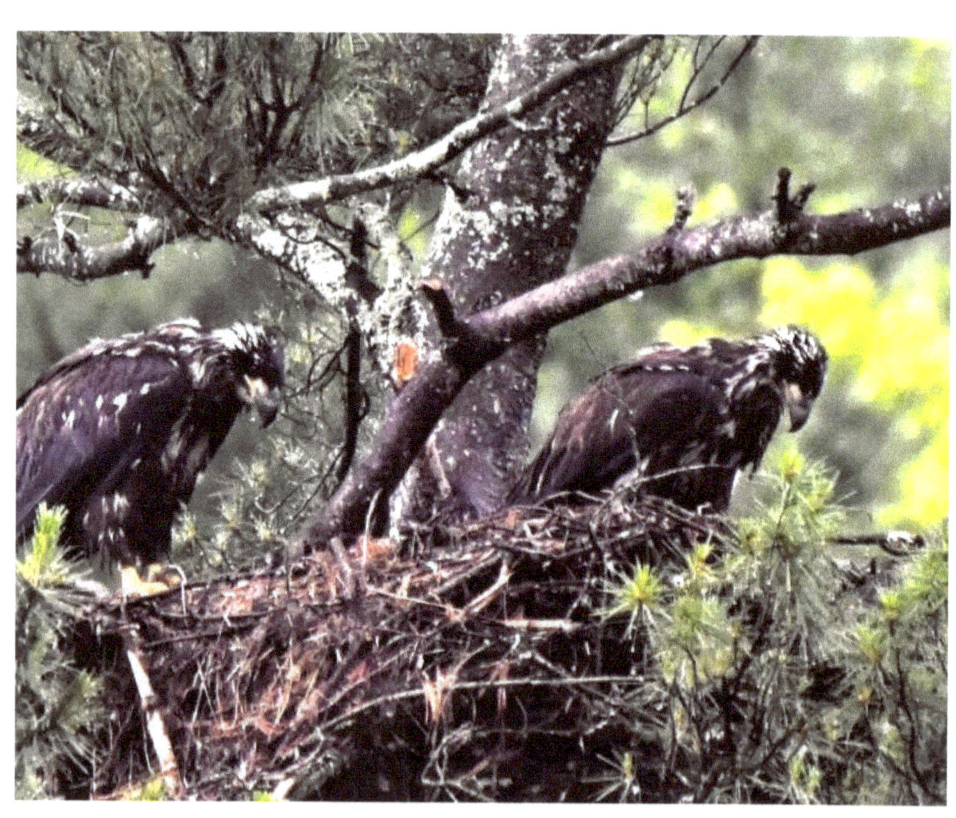

Eaglet Dreams

Remember when you and your sibling
used to sit on the porch together
counting Chevys and Fords?

Not quite ready to fly away,
but knowing something big
was about to happen.

Watching the world go by
without worry, or hunger, or fear.
Living in the moment

with your best friend in the world.
Your only friend in the world.
Before your heads turned white.

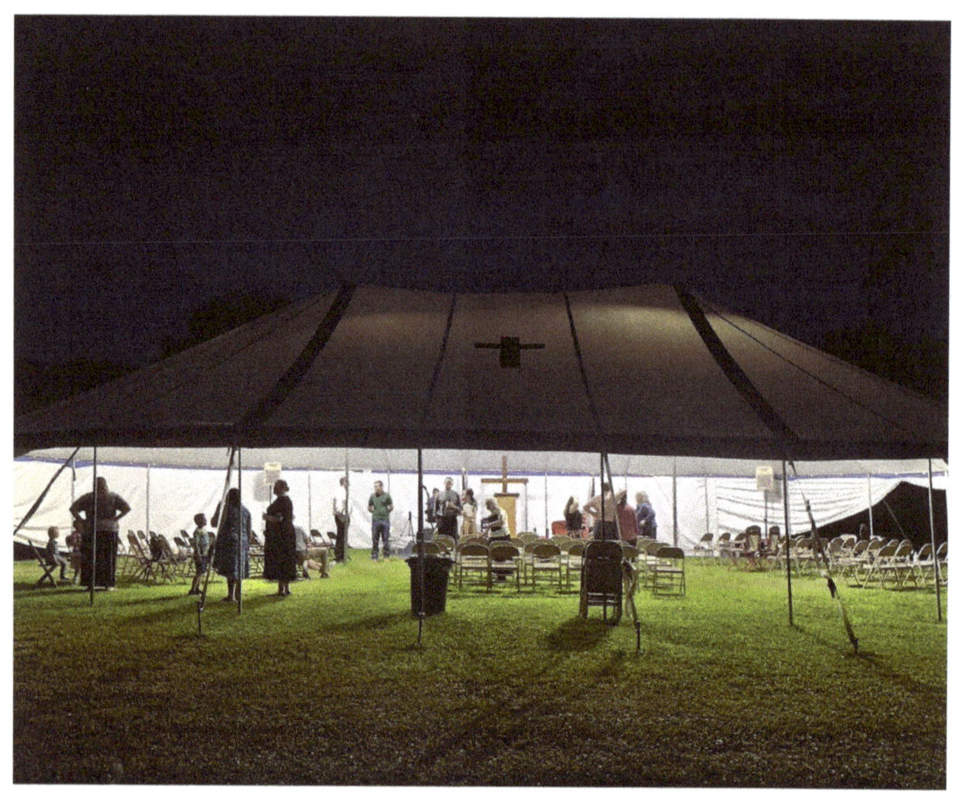

Unrepentant

I used to drink coffee
with Johnny Paycheck
while visiting the
Ohio personal care home
he briefly shared
with my Mamaw.

Dozens of working class
records earned him a fortune.
Booze, coke, and the IRS
took most of it.
After shooting a stranger
in a shabby, run-down beer joint,
Johnny served a hitch
in the Chillicothe, Ohio penituary.

Haggard helped with legal fees.
Jerry Lee Lewis did a benefit concert.
Willie successfully lobbied
 for an early medical release.
The emphysema took him
at the age of 64.
Ole George Jones paid for
the burial plot, right
 beside his own in Nashville.
At the funeral, a dozen
 Hell's Angels sat in
pews filled with
gray pony tails, crooked noses,
Carhartt, Earnhardt, and leather,
ushered across the aisle from the Pagans.
A brief bond forged through
solidarity over Paycheck.

If Johnny had been
a comic-book hero
he would have been Wolverine:
short, mean, and quick to rile.
Sober and Saved
at the end, he
shared no regrets.
He expressed no remorse.
Despite the constant chaos, he always insisted,

*"I'm basically a pretty level-headed guy."*

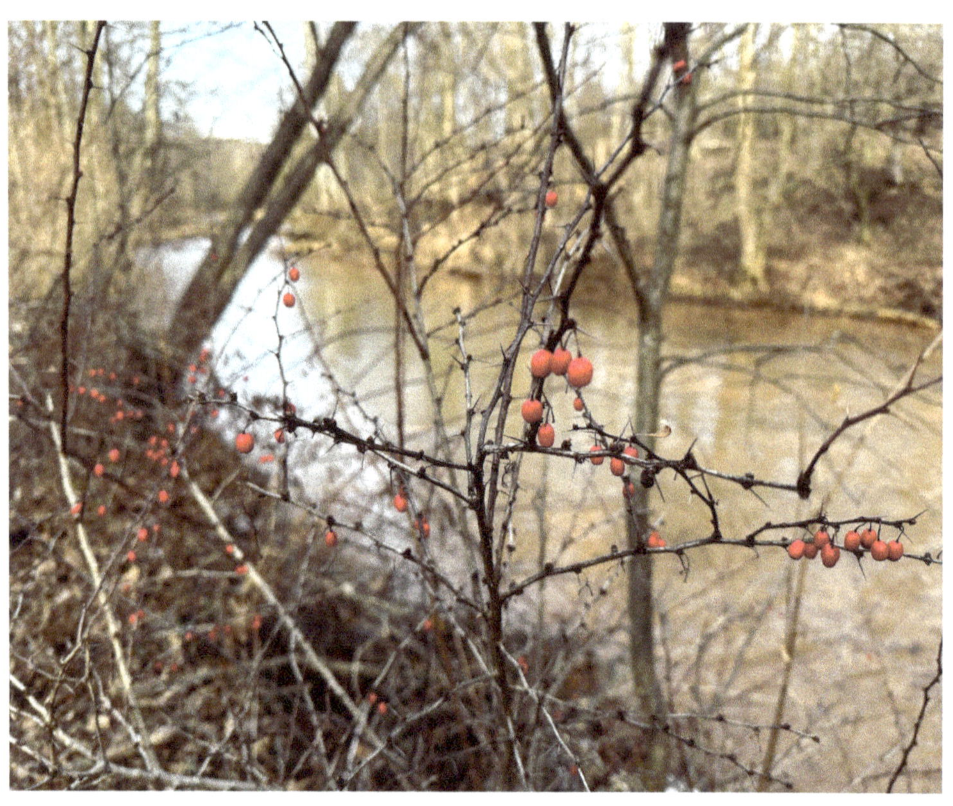

Deer Hunt Haiku

Up on Fiddlers Run
barberries burn a glowing red.
Waiting for the snow

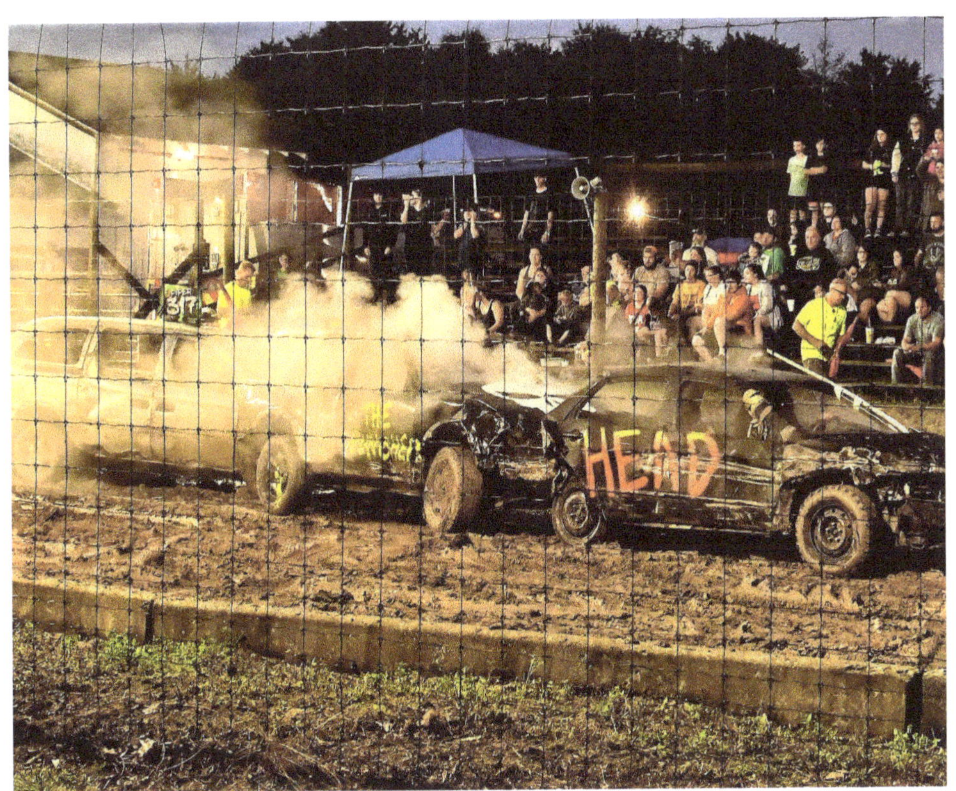


Iron Horse

On I-95 south in a torrential rain,
a fully leathered, helmetless,
aviator goggled biker appears
riding a flat-black,
stripped down Panhead,
speeding full-bore in
the far left passing lane,
eyes straight ahead,
impenetrable to the
cold, wet, the misery.
No radio, no cruise control,
no windshield, no conversation.
Focused, unflinching, resolute,
Riding toward a direction,
not a destination.

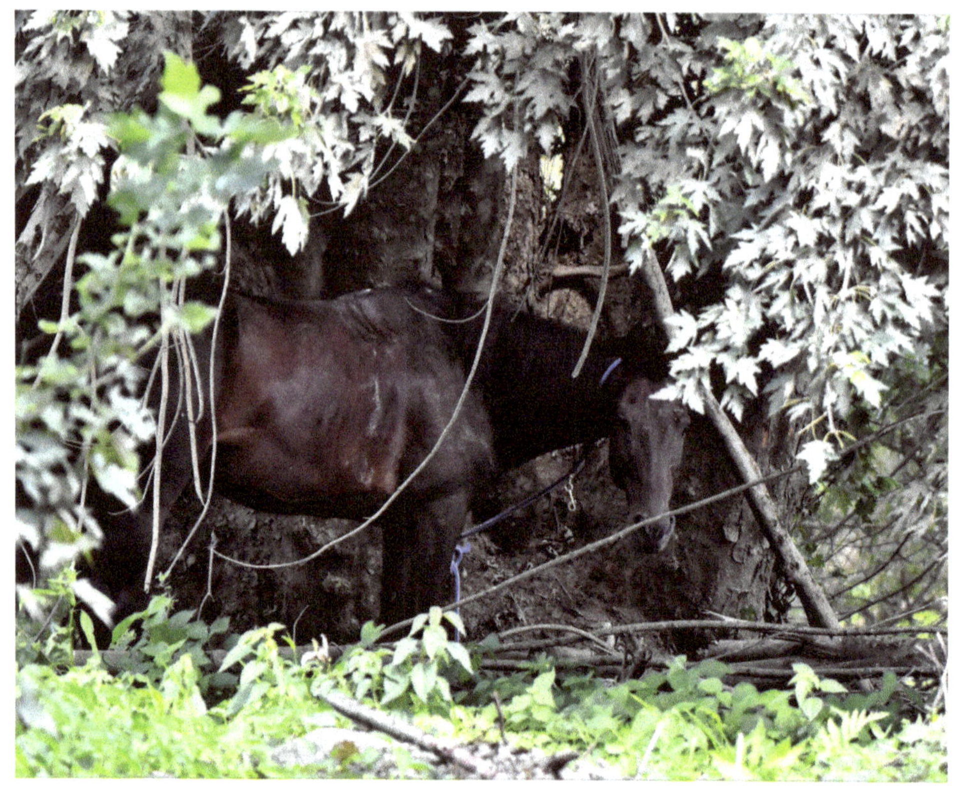

Mabel

Mabel was a dutiful, 25-year-old, coal black,
Shire, the tallest of the draft horse breeds.
My great-uncle bought her from a neighbor
from up on Clutts' Hill, led her 10 miles
over Union Ridge, down Crab Run, and
up to the head of the holler on Turkey Creek.
Her final destination.

When I was 9 years old, maybe 10,
I visited our old plow horse
in the hot summer evenings and
sprayed her with a toxic DDT infused mixture
from a plunger attached to a metal canister,
holding my breath until I saw stars.

I swatted billows of tormenting horse flies.
Poor Mabel constantly swished her tail and
stomped her hind legs up and down, scattering
those green-headed demons.
It seemed so hopeless, truly futile--- at least to me.
Yet she remained calm and serene.
Or overwhelmed.

Mable grew friendly with me.
She would mosey up to the pasture gate as I approached and
nuzzle my closed fist holding treats:
apple slices, carrot bits, celery, and peppermint candy.
Then one evening, I climbed over the wooden gate
grabbed her mane, up onto her bare back.
She hated to be ridden. I knew that.

I had betrayed Mabel's trust.
She tolerated me on her back a few more times,
then no longer greeted me.
Offers of apples, treats, and
horse fly swats were scorned.
I was scorned.

One evening, a few feet out of reach,
she eyed me with:
What a little jerk you turned out to be.
She was right, of course.
Six decades later, I think of Mabel
with lingering remorse and regret.

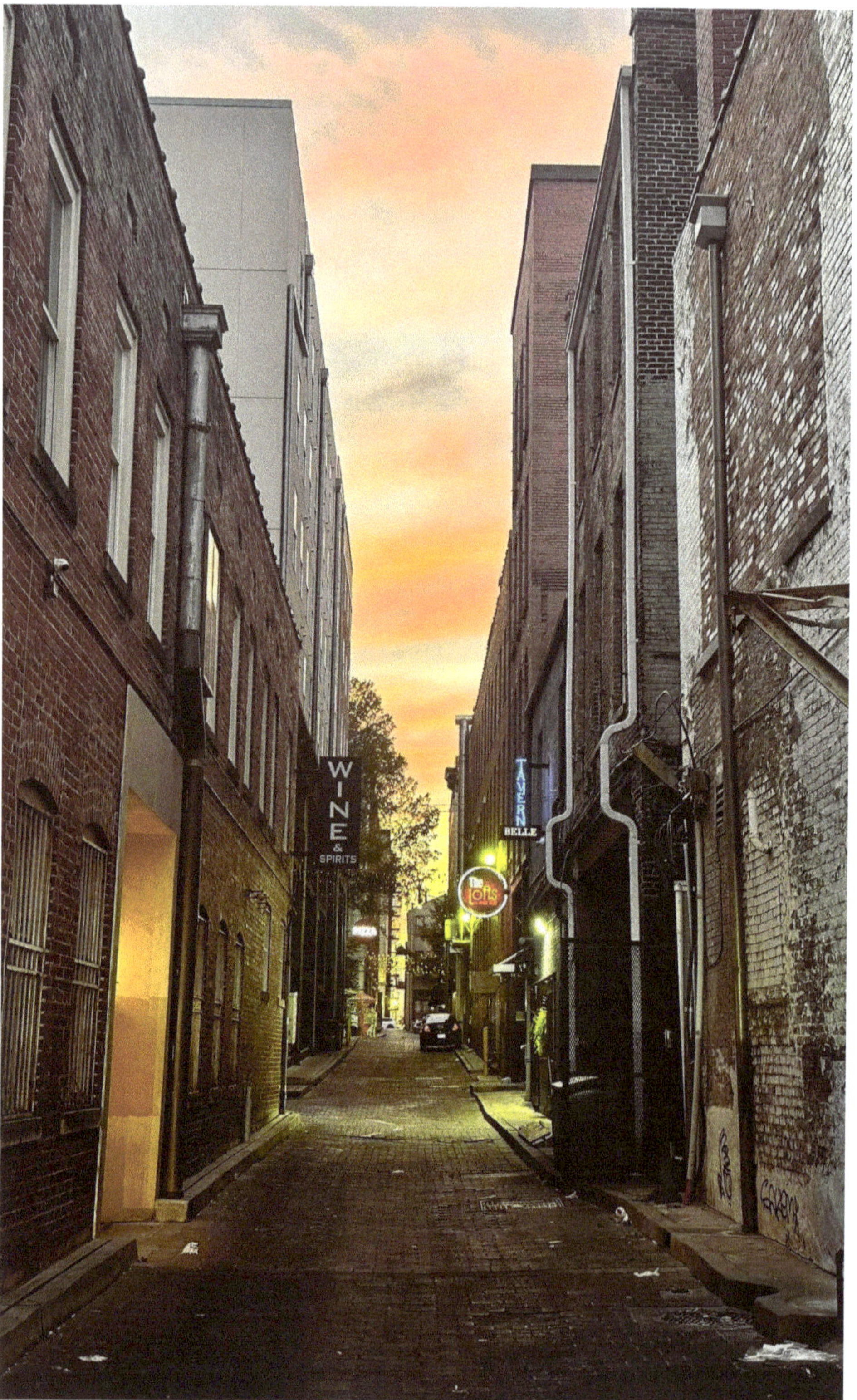

WINE & SPIRITS
TAVERN
BELLE
The Lofts

Kansas City Star

In a squeezed Kansas City
sweatbox bar with
sawdust floors and
long, vintage shuffleboard table,
Sade's *Smooth Operator*
drops on the jukebox.

My barstool neighbor
saunters onto the dance floor
grabbing the oldest uncle
in the room.
She is hypnotic. Mesmerizing.
Peroxide blond hair
piled high.
Pack of Kools
peeking from her bra.
Short, clingy sun dress.
Jailhouse tattoo below her neck:
*Built to last.*

The whole room watches her dance.
Assured, earthy, unaffected.
Indifferent to everyone and everything
but the pulse of
that soothing salsa rhythm.
We watch her transform into a poem,
each movement a word.

40 years later,
when I hear Sade's voice
I feel the steamy heat and
see that sultry sway.
*No need to ask---*
*She's a smooth operator......*

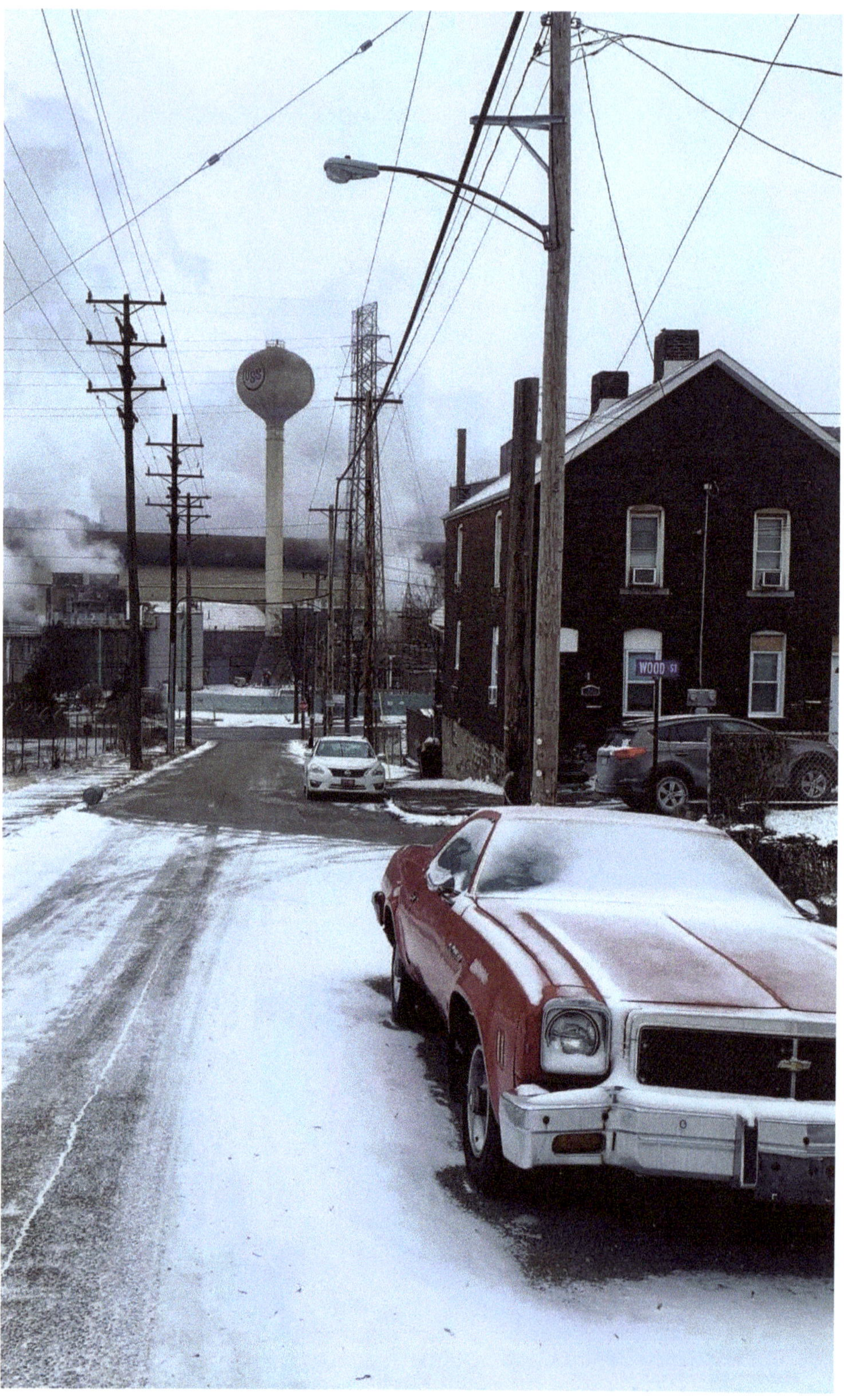

USS
WOOD ST

(One) Last Time
*Inspired by Robert Earl Keen's "Dreadful Selfish Crime"*

Seems like yesterday
that coming and going
didn't matter much.
Until I no longer could.
She stopped by, unannounced,
for a short trip
to a far-away place.
We ignored the mirror
reflecting our missed chances
and the flinches that
had rebuilt our faces.
Our pasts nothing
but stray cats
roaming unleashed
through the alleys
of our memories,
reminders of our
impermanent passion,
lingering sorrow,
and unfinished regret.

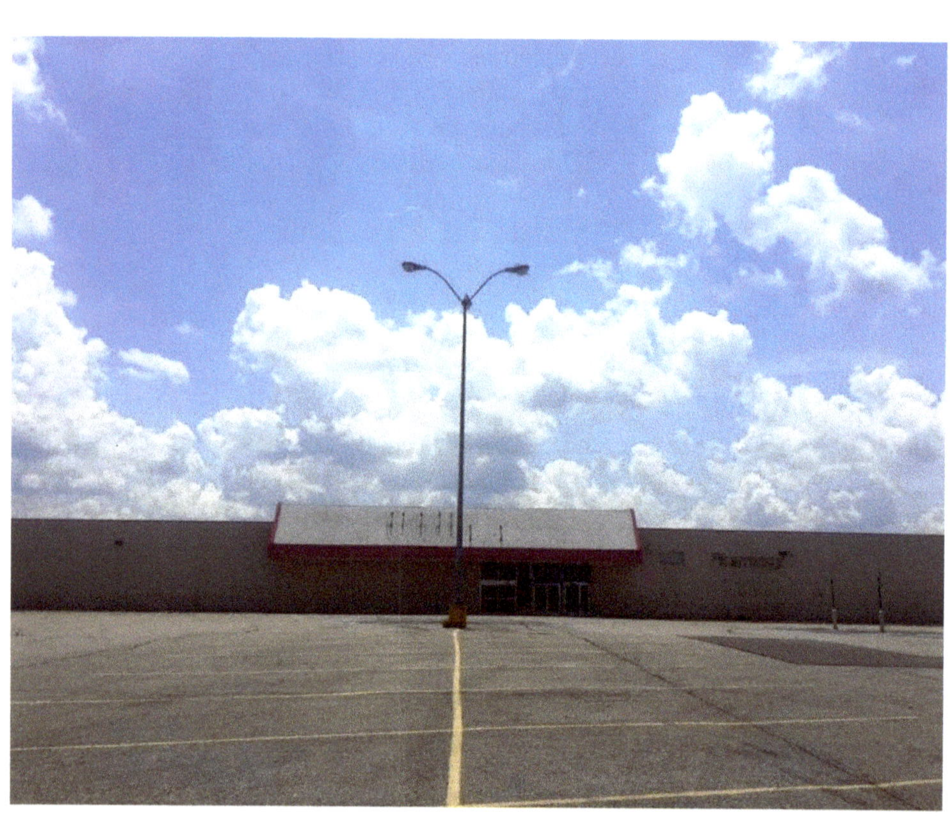

Introvert Hell

Sitting in the dealership waiting room
while my truck gets serviced,
new Vonnegut book in hand.
An older than me dude (#1)
loudly talks nonstop
to anyone who
makes the mistake of
looking his way.

For a brief minute
it is only the two of us.
His comments to me are
met with armored-up
one word responses.
I am in introvert hell.

Another older guy (#2)
takes a seat.
They engage in what
can only be described as
two monologues in
search of a dialogue:

#1— *my wife passed away 6 years ago and I couldn't stand staying in our house, so I moved up here.*
　　　*#2— I should've made myself some breakfast.*
#1— *I'm getting my knee replaced in 2 weeks.*
　　　*#2— My grandson is in high school and works a full time job and a part-time job.*
And on it went.

A line then jumps out from my book:
*Be soft, do not let the world make you hard.*

The door swings open:
*Mr. Clary, your truck is ready.*

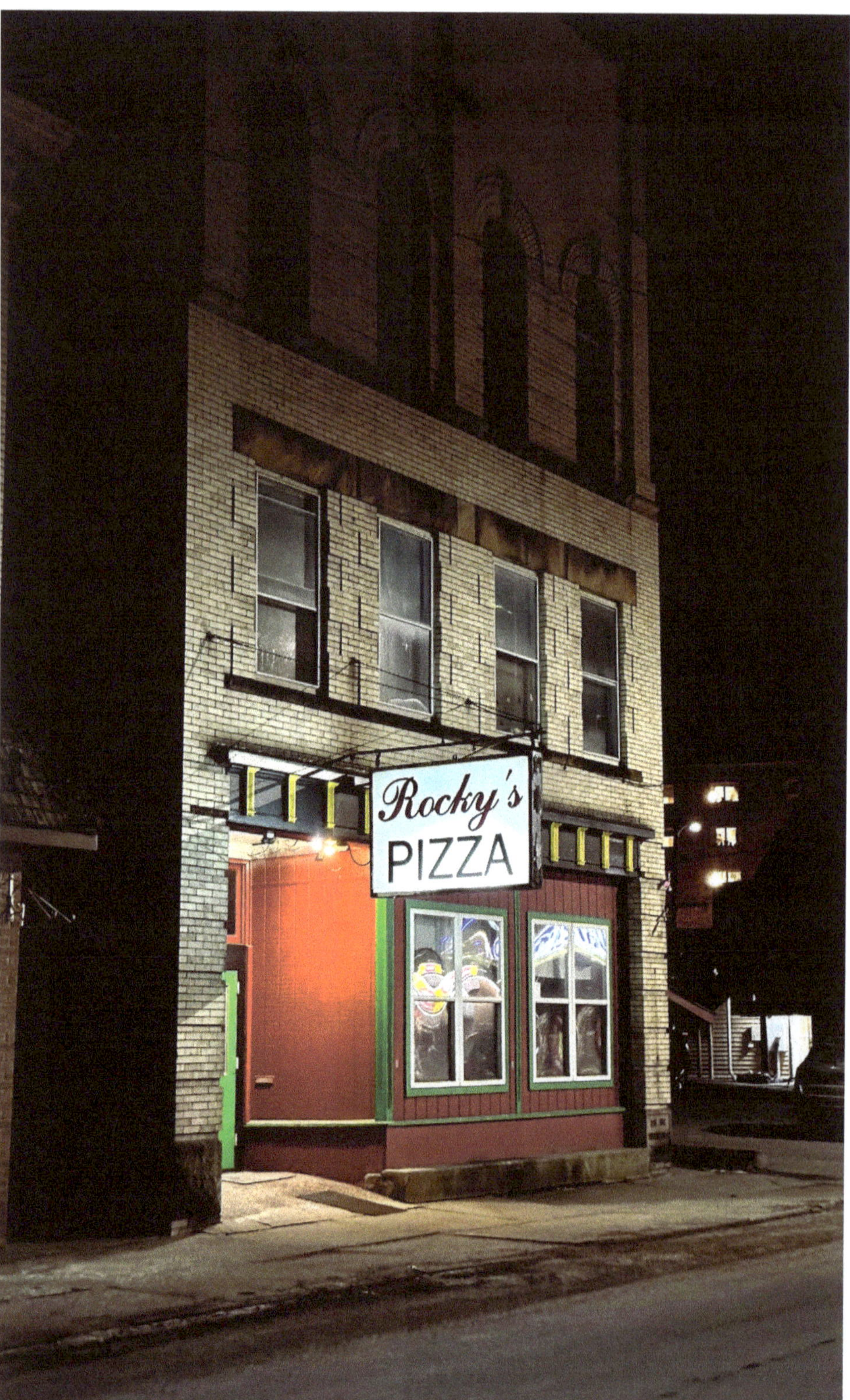
Rocky's
PIZZA

Thinking Outside the Bar

Her name is Tina,
petite, hair piled high
B-hive style, but not sprayed.
Lipstick thick, pale blue.
Efficient, perceptive, competent.
Friendly, but not too friendly.
A compelling woman,
who stays cool and in control.

I ask, *Where did you grow up?*
*Around here,* she replies.
When I praise her bar skills,
she studies me and says,
*I have been doing this*
*for 13 years. I'm done.*
*I want to go back to school for nursing.*
*Before it's too late.*

I point out her transferable skills:
Serving the public, meeting high demands,
working the nightshift, dispensing potions,
getting underpaid, handling jag-offs.

She pauses, *Yeah, and watch you drink.*
*Funny, how I get tipped for keeping your glass filled and*
*nurses receive nothing for keeping you alive.*
*But, for once, I am following hope.*

We lock eyes and she spins away.
What'll you have fellas?
Happy Hour ends in 10 minutes.

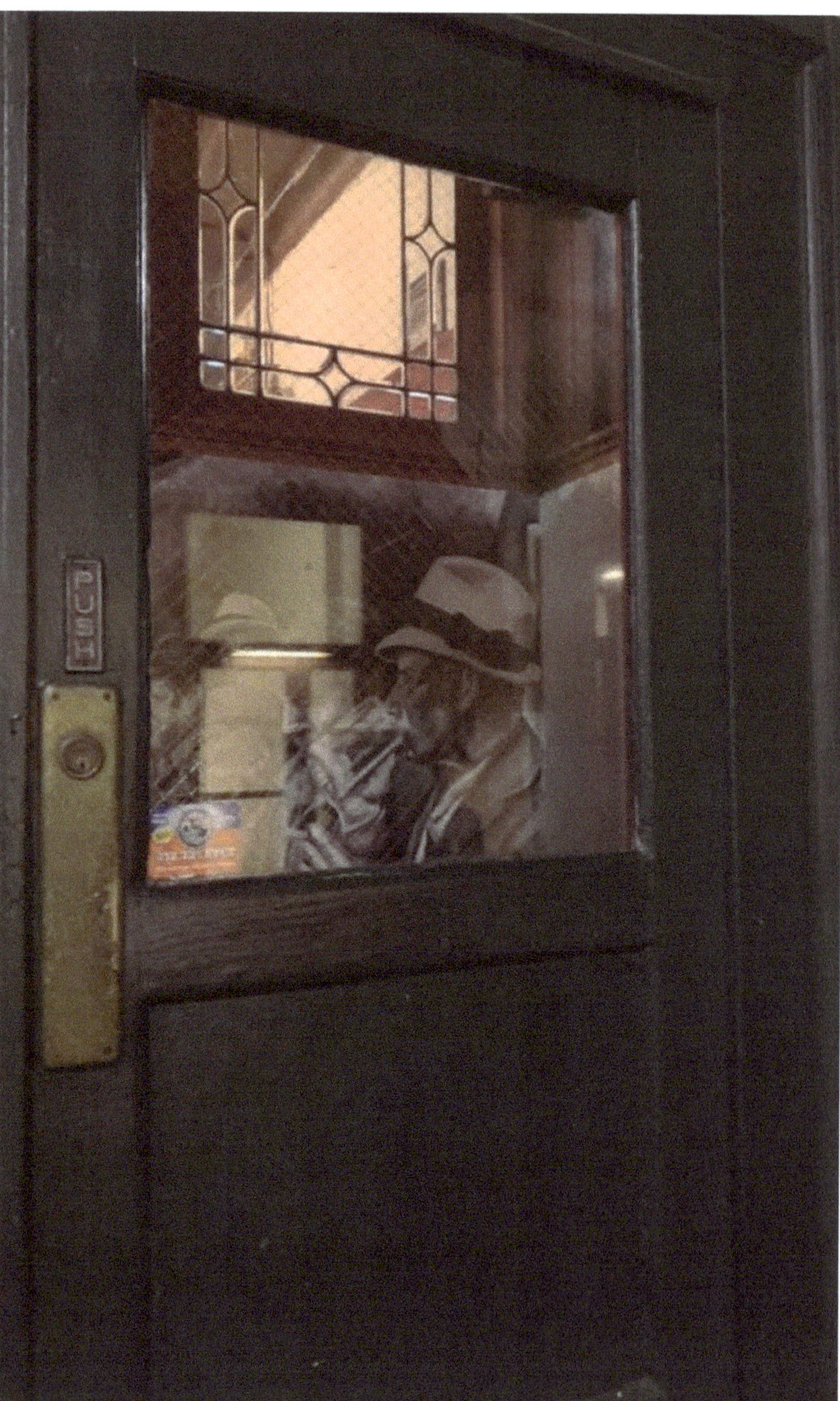

After Dark, Before Dawn

Fifty years ago tonight,
New Year's Eve, 1971
Fourth Avenue in Huntington, West Virginia,
was busy. Drivers circled the block
looking for parking places.
Stores were dark, beer joints were packed.
Carousers filled the streets.

Inside the swank Elephant Walk,
a venerable bartender, Zion Turner,
resplendent in his white linen jacket,
shook martinis, lit customer's cigarettes,
then dusted the bar of its loose piles of greenbacks.

The band played:
*"You know where to find her,
Just follow the sign.
Dining and dancing,
Cocktails and wine."* (1)

Yet, tonight, the words Del sang ring true:
*"Night still falls but
It doesn't make a sound."* (2)

(1) *Leona* by Stonewall Jackson
(2) *Mill Towns* by Del McCoury

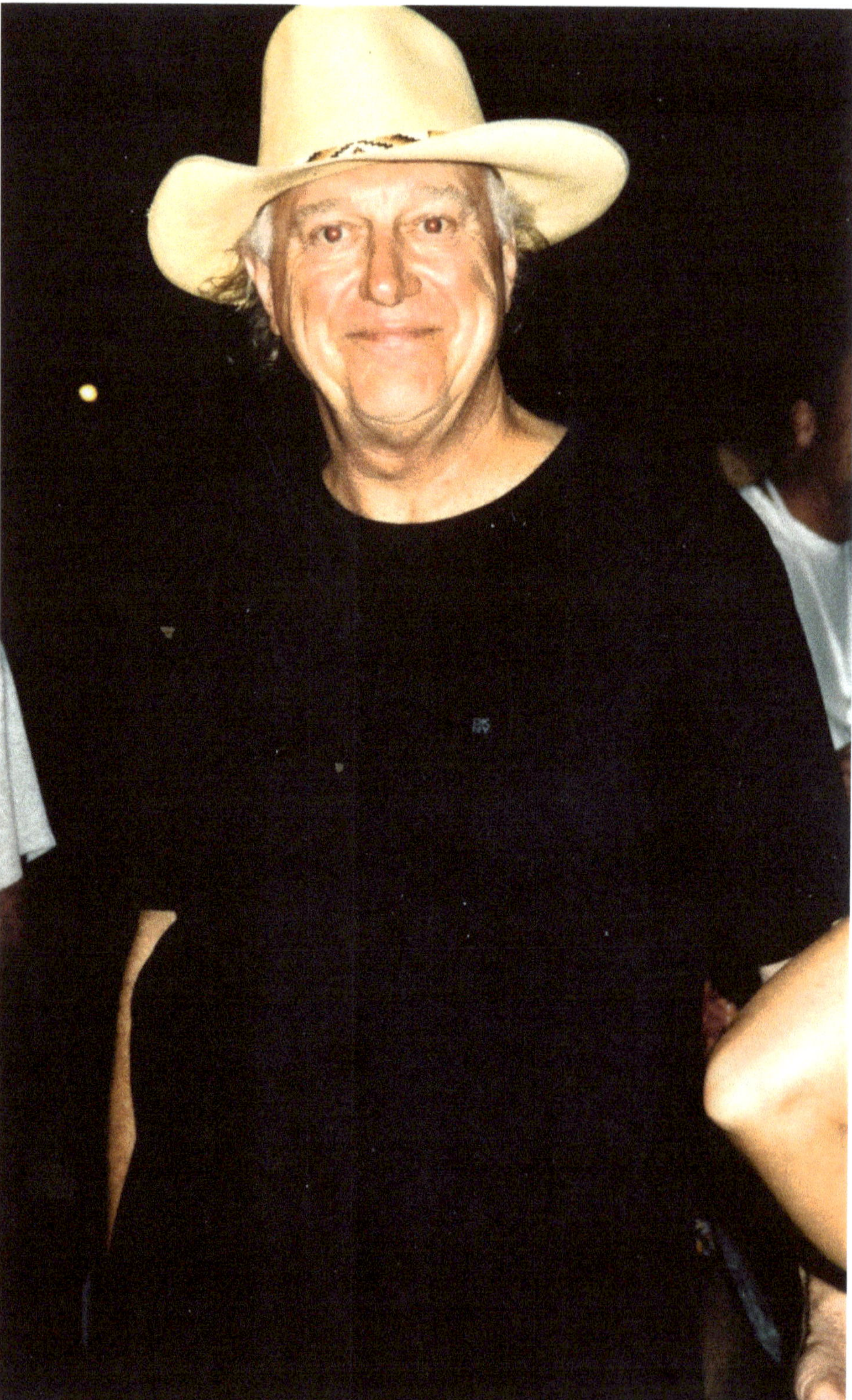

Drinking with Jerry Jeff

*You can't do anything again, but
you can do something similar.*

Jerry Jeff told me that over a cold Belikin
at Pedro's in Ambergris Caye.

He told me a lot of things:
*I don't take requests, only suggestions.*

*Bojangles is played different every night
'cause I hate singalongs.*

The first show was with Willie, in Huntington, WV.
Then Pittsburgh, NYC, Austin, Alexandia,

Akron, Gruene Hall, a private party in Erie, and
this, a week in Belize.

He leaned in and rumbled,
*Anything worth doing*

*is worth overdoing.
Tonight, anyway.*

An admiring Deliah stopped by
and said, *You're the Man!*

He laughed that laugh and shot back,
*Well, somebody has to be The Man.*

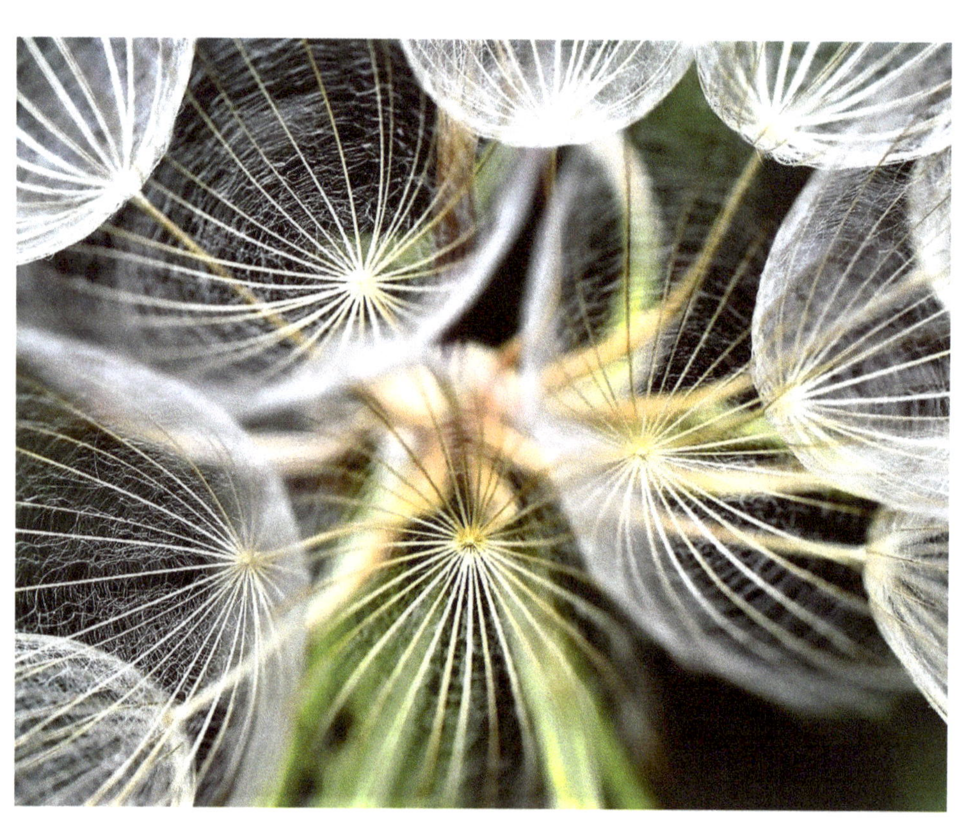

She Wrote Maya Angelou

She wrote Maya Angelou
a lipstick note on my mirror
thanking her for the reminder to believe me
the first time I showed her
who I was.

Deception reflects
lack of understanding,
yet discerning the truth
demands belief.

Oscar Wilde declared that
*Deceiving others is called romance.*
my lipstick reply on the mirror to
you and Ms. Angelou.

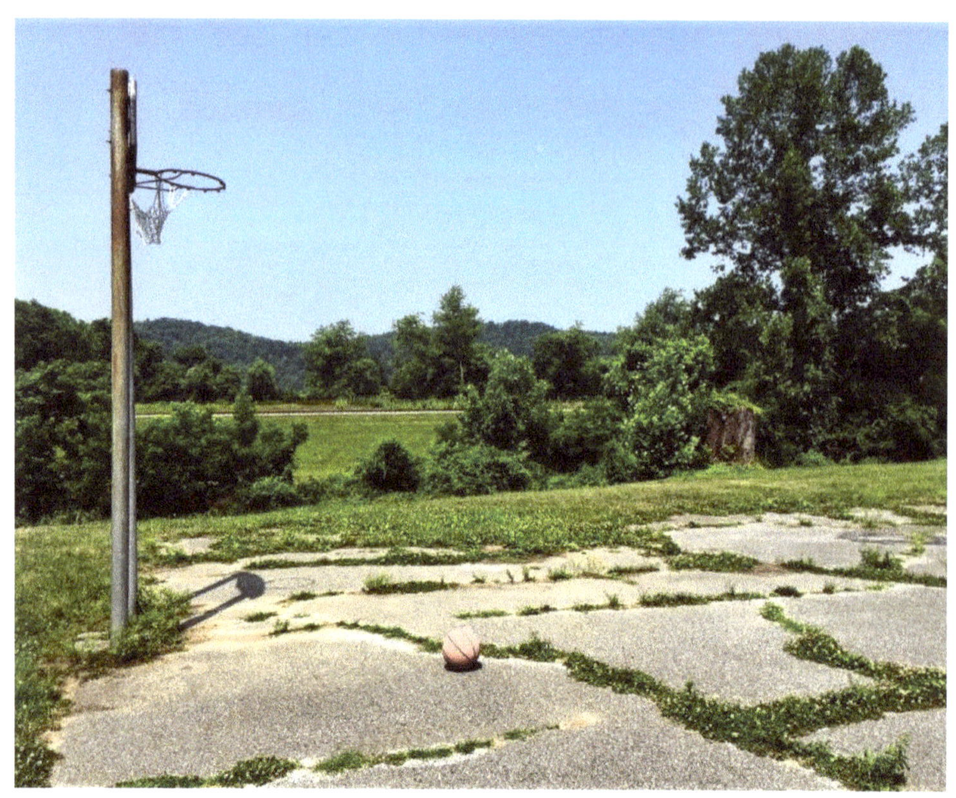

Playground Ghosts

Lots of good memories
with lots of old friends

I can still hear their voices
ghosts laughing
in the bright daylight.

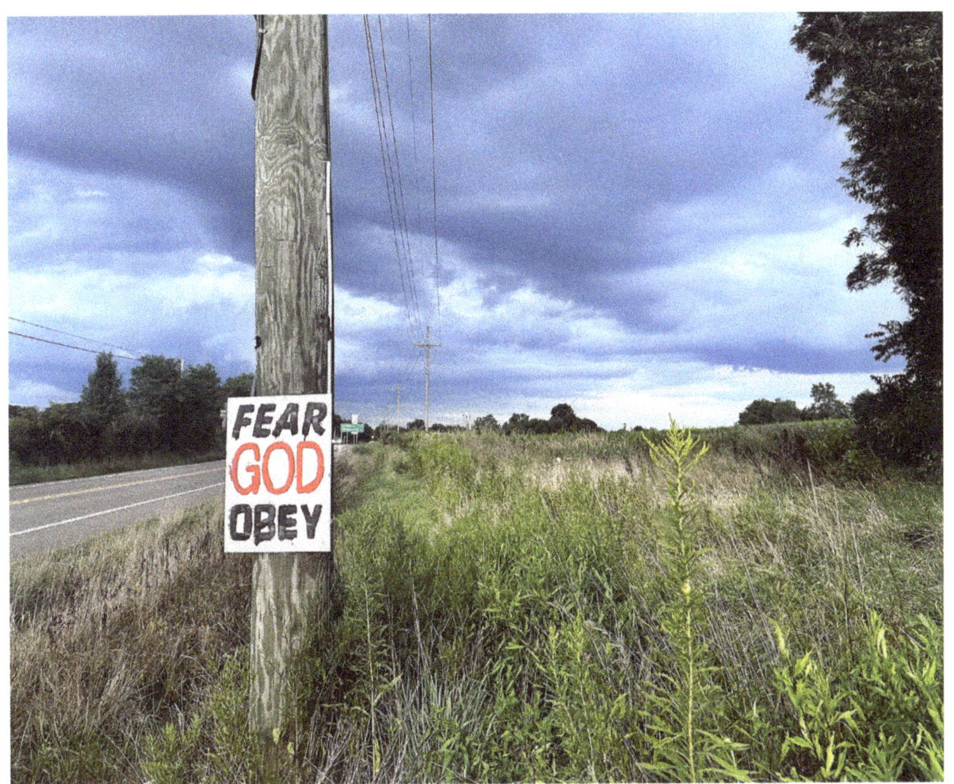


Time to Sing

My old friend Harlan
has been in the hospital
for 5 months
where he now floats
in a morphine dream.

Today, I visited Harlan
when, out of the blue,
he began singing,
*Dust on the Bible.*

I never knew Harlan
to attend church
or even hum a melody but
now, as the blinds close,
this old Hank Williams song
untroubles his suffering.

Mysterious thing— dying.
I wonder what curveballs
I'll be slinging
when my turn comes
to change worlds?

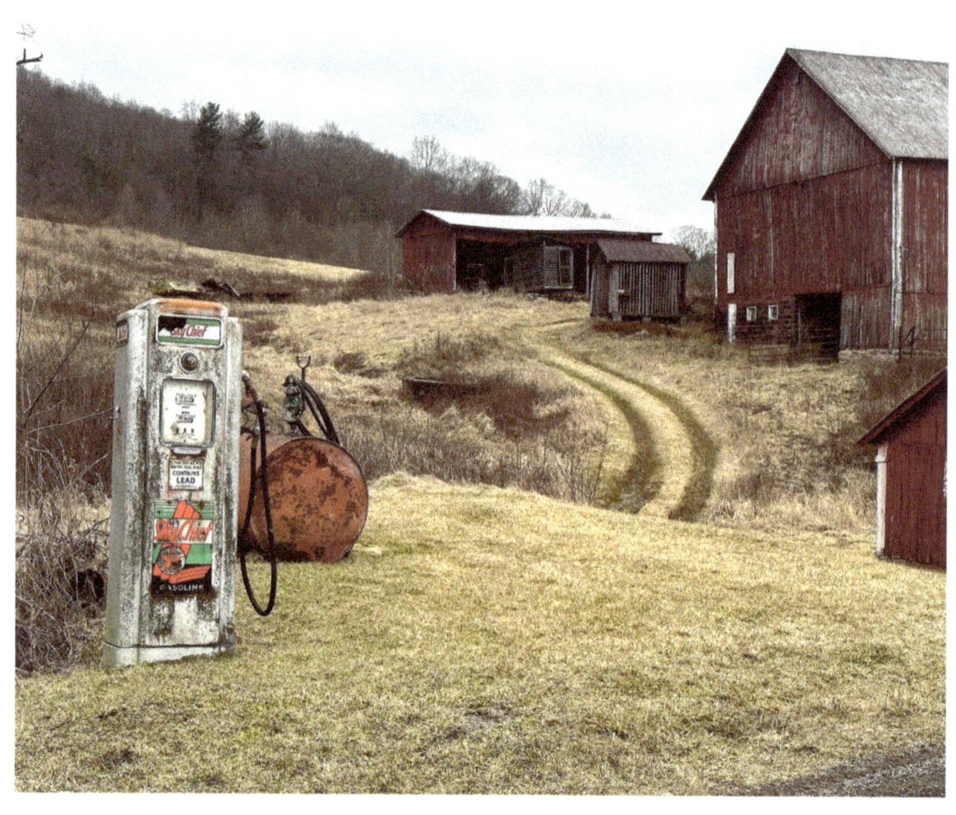

Tell Me a Story

*Are you Patty's boy?*, the old man asks
during my visit back home.
*Sure am*, I answer.
My mother died 67 years ago.
I am 70 years old and still called Patty's boy.


Shared memories and stories
strengthen our social ties.
Yet, community bonds are unraveling.
Our interactions are fading.
Others no longer know who we belong to.
We are losing our collective memories.


What if our stories are never learned?
How can we trust each other if
we don't know each other?
We used to sit till bedtime sharing tales and memories.
And the kids listened, keeping memories alive.
Now we share our stories with paid strangers---
lawyers, therapists, insurance adjusters, the police,
and sit till bedtime
zooming the grandkids,
texting our friends,
binge watching Netflix on the TV.

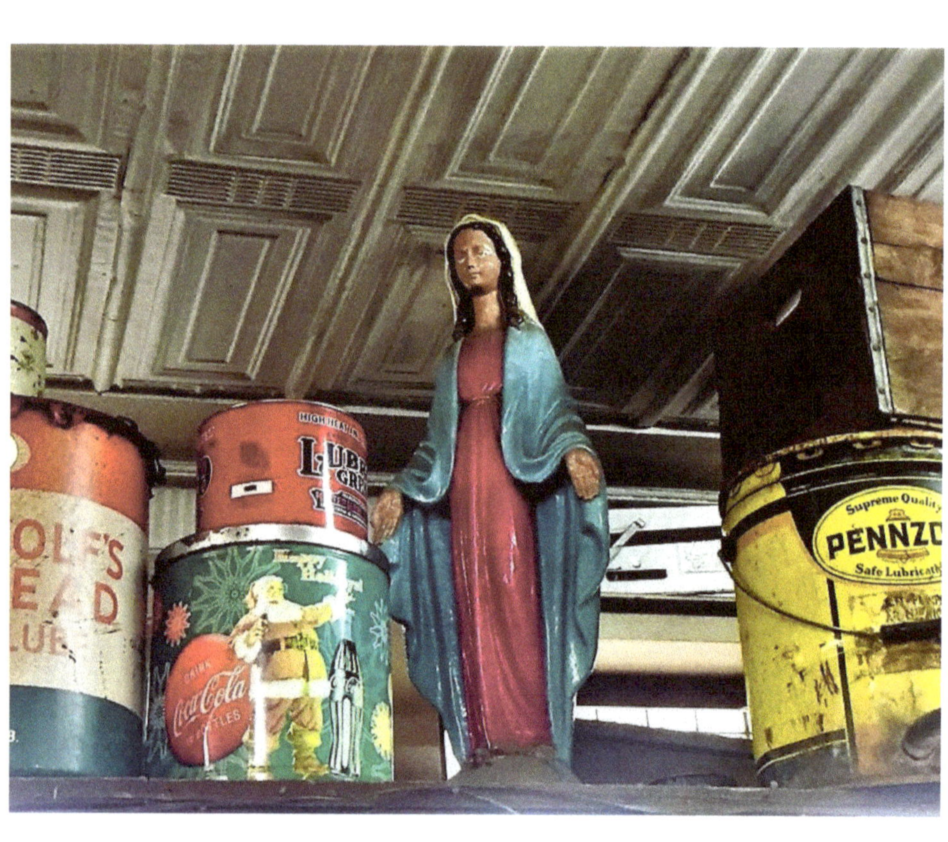
OLF'S
EAD
LUB
B.
HIGH HEAT
LUBE
GRE
DRINK
Coca-Cola
BOTTLES
Supreme Quality
PENNZ
Safe Lubricati

Impresarios of Memory

It all ends up here at the flea market.
Your Marvel comics,
knick-knack owl collection,
avocado colored fondue set.
The brown furniture your kids don't want.

There was a time when flea markets thrilled me.
A treasure hunt with foreseen haggling.
Lessons learned, not instructed.

*Do any better than $15.00 on this Fiesta plate?*
        *Sure---how about $20.00?*

Once, while eying an ornate iron bed frame,
The seller offered to take it apart.
*You know,* he said, *I like things made of metal.*
*Used to you'd throw your lard bucket into the creek*
*and it would rust up and go right on back to dirt.*
*That old plastic stuff won't do that.*

The vendors: each an independent boss, skilled in
marketing, product knowledge, rapport building,
telling funny stories, reading body language,
the ability to close the deal.

I touch things that have wonderful stories behind them,
forever lost but readily imagined.
I touch things that bring back personal memories:
a blue Shirley Temple pitcher like the one in Mamaw's kitchen,
a Big Red Machine pennant from their 1970s glory years,
a Falls City beer sign, once ubiquitous in every West Virginia bar, and
a set of Bobbsey Twins books, the same ones I read in grade school.

In the end it's all just stuff.
Cultural artifacts that represent
moments of our personal life story.
Moments that are forgotten and
unnoticed until their meaning
is revealed by these flea market
*Impresarios of Memory.*

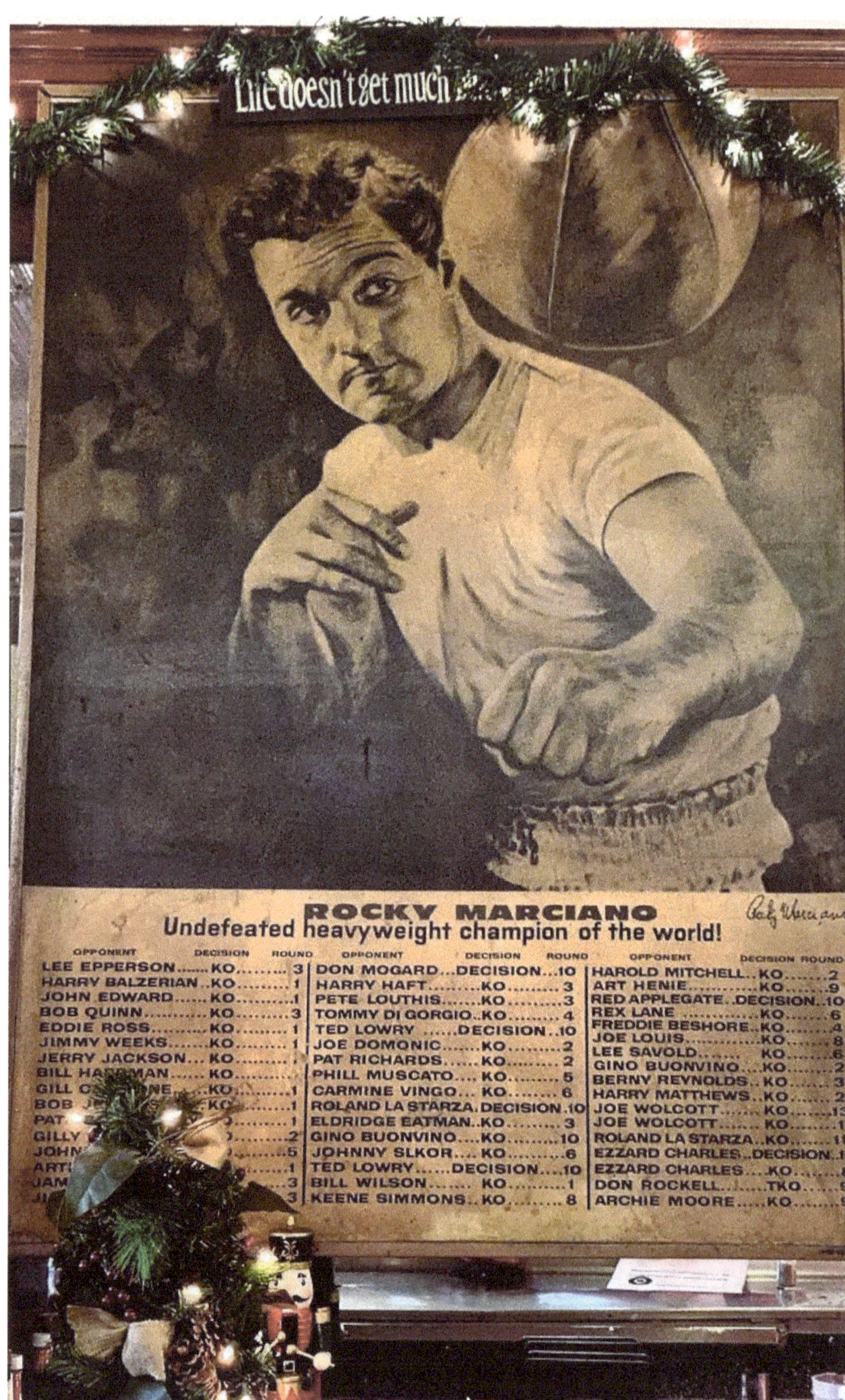


| OPPONENT | DECISION | ROUND | OPPONENT | DECISION | ROUND | OPPONENT | DECISION | ROUND |
|---|---|---|---|---|---|---|---|---|
| LEE EPPERSON | KO | 3 | DON MOGARD | DECISION | 10 | HAROLD MITCHELL | KO | 2 |
| HARRY BALZERIAN | KO | 1 | HARRY HAFT | KO | 3 | ART HENIE | KO | 9 |
| JOHN EDWARD | KO | 1 | PETE LOUTHIS | KO | 3 | RED APPLEGATE | DECISION | 10 |
| BOB QUINN | KO | 3 | TOMMY DI GORGIO | KO | 4 | REX LANE | KO | 6 |
| EDDIE ROSS | KO | 1 | TED LOWRY | DECISION | 10 | FREDDIE BESHORE | KO | 4 |
| JIMMY WEEKS | KO | 1 | JOE DOMONIC | KO | 2 | JOE LOUIS | KO | 8 |
| JERRY JACKSON | KO |  | PAT RICHARDS | KO | 2 | LEE SAVOLD | KO | 6 |
| BILL HARDMAN | KO |  | PHILL MUSCATO | KO | 5 | GINO BUONVINO | KO | 2 |
| GILL CARDIONE | KO | 1 | CARMINE VINGO | KO | 6 | BERNY REYNOLDS | KO | 3 |
| BOB JEFFERSON | KO | 1 | ROLAND LA STARZA | DECISION | 10 | HARRY MATTHEWS | KO | 2 |
| PAT | | 1 | ELDRIDGE EATMAN | KO | 3 | JOE WOLCOTT | KO | 13 |
| GILLY | | 2 | GINO BUONVINO | KO | 10 | JOE WOLCOTT | KO | 1 |
| JOHN | | 5 | JOHNNY SLKOR | KO | 6 | ROLAND LA STARZA | KO | 11 |
| ART | | 1 | TED LOWRY | DECISION | 10 | EZZARD CHARLES | DECISION | 15 |
| JAM | | 3 | BILL WILSON | KO | 1 | EZZARD CHARLES | KO | 8 |
| JIM | | 3 | KEENE SIMMONS | KO | 8 | DON ROCKELL | TKO | 9 |
| | | | | | | ARCHIE MOORE | KO | 9 |

Iron City Christmas

Having a fish sandwich
and Iron City at
Pittsburgh's oldest bar, the
Original Oyster House.

150 years on the same corner.
No frills, one page menu,
recipes 100 years old.
Cash only.

My wife asks: *Do you
have any Hendrick's gin?*

*Nope—Gordons and Gilbey's.
Tanqueray sometimes.*

It's the Tuesday night before Christmas.
Outside the door, Pittsburgh's
seasonal Holiday Village
has taken over Market Square.

Kiosks selling distinctive ethnic
Christmas ornaments fill the area.
Ukranian tree balls, Celtic trinity knots,
Bavarian Santas, Kenyan soapstone stars.

Behind the bar hangs a huge, faded
poster of Rocky Marciano,
with all 49 fights listed
below his Christmas wreathed picture.

Undefeated and still
Heavyweight Champion of the World.
Festooned with colored lights, his right arm cocked,
ready to knock you out.

As I step back to the restroom,
I hear the bartender say to the cook:

*Hey Jigsy, you fucked up.*

Jigsy stops and stiffens with
*I fucked up the day I started working here.*

I paused, caught his eye, and said,
*Merry Christmas, Jigsy.*

He shrugged with a
*Merry Christmas, my man.*

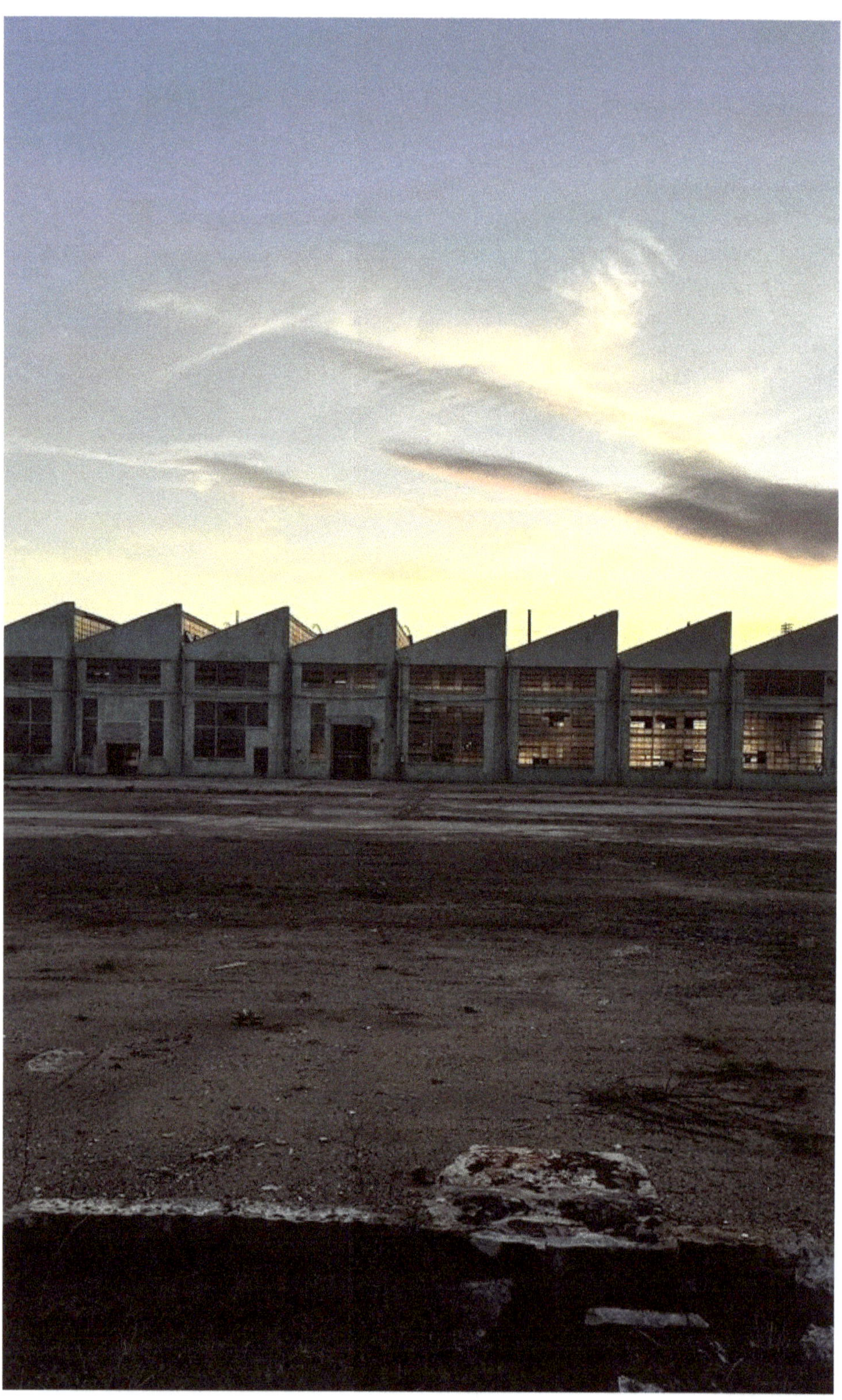

Charm

A college girlfriend once
told me that
being a horse's ass
was part of my charm.
The only time
I can recall
my name and
the word charm
spoken in
the same sentence.

Nosey the Cat contently kneads
my chest as she
purrs like a gentle breeze on my lap.

A rumpled toothless toddler at Sheetz
grins and readily offers up
her sticky, gummy, lollipop.

My great-aunt Jessie indulges me
with her iron skillet cornbread
whenever I visit.

All so unaware
of my true essence
hidden beneath a mask.
A silent presence amid deep shadows

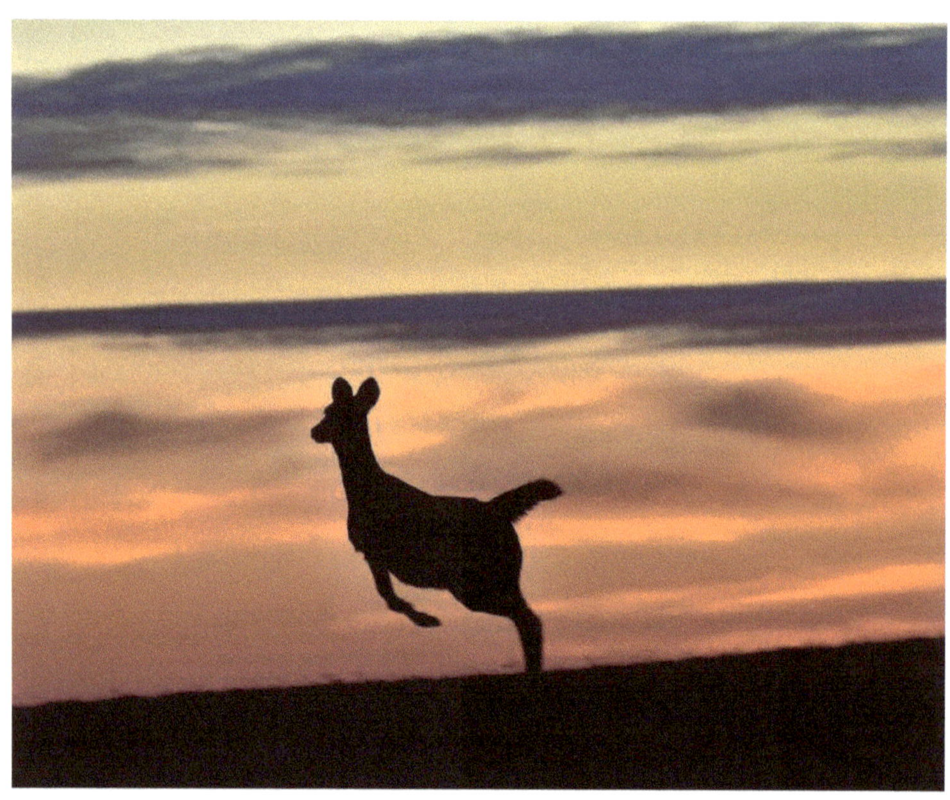

Deer Season

Changes are coming.
Cooler air,
red summer coats swapped
for brown winter furs.
Human scent
now sparking fear,
not curiosity

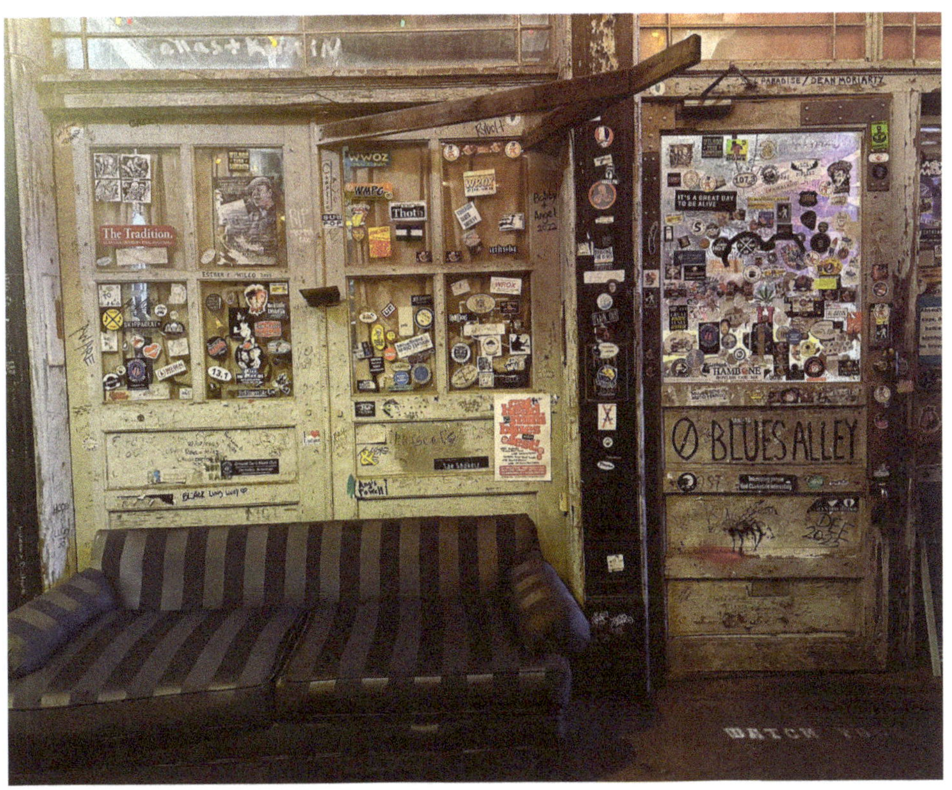


Down at Rachael's

To the *jag-off*
at the bar
during old man
dollar-drafts-hour,
sipping on a glass
of stale white wine,
yapping on speakerphone
to your pansy cousin
whose stolen
Range Rover ended up
incinerated on TikTok:

*Take it outside!*

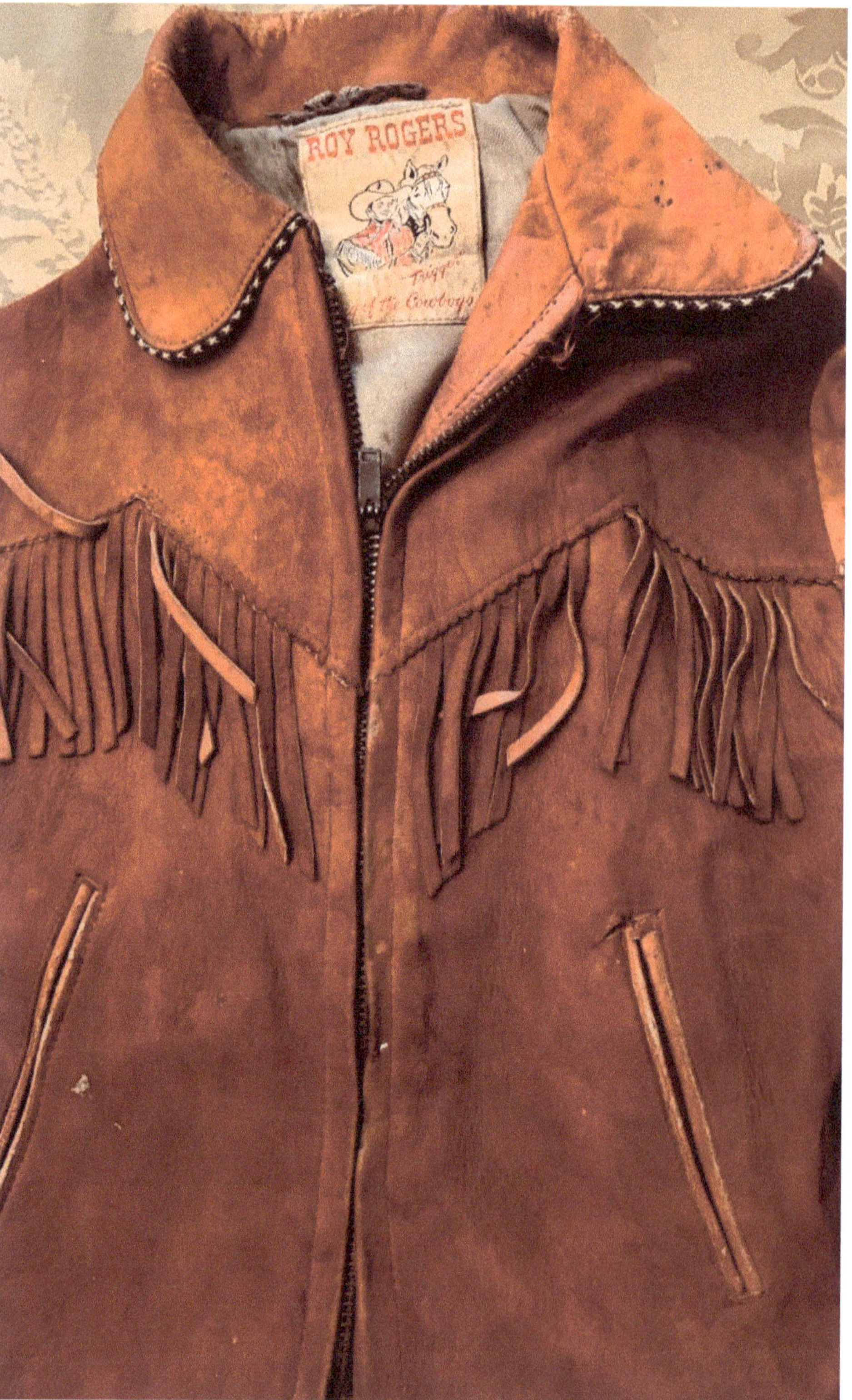
ROY ROGERS
Trigg
of the Cowboys

# 1959

Started first grade and
met my life-long best friend,
who cried and cried. Then
he never cried again.

Rode the bus, carried a
zoo animals lunch bucket,
nibbled on evergreen paste,
watched Popeye cartoons,
got a buzz cut every 2 weeks.
and every Sunday, I learned
that Hell was Hot.

Peed my pants when I
was downtown with my
Mamaw, afraid to ask,
Where's the bathroom?

Spent weekends on
Turkey Creek, learned to
make a slingshot, and
helped butcher hogs
on Thanksgiving Day.

For Christmas, got a
transistor radio, outer
space ray gun, and
a Roy Rogers fringed jacket.

People called me "Patty's Boy",
followed by, *So sad she
died so young. How old
were you? Three?*

I lived up a holler,
knew all my neighbors.
Loved them all and
they loved me.

1960 came much
too soon.

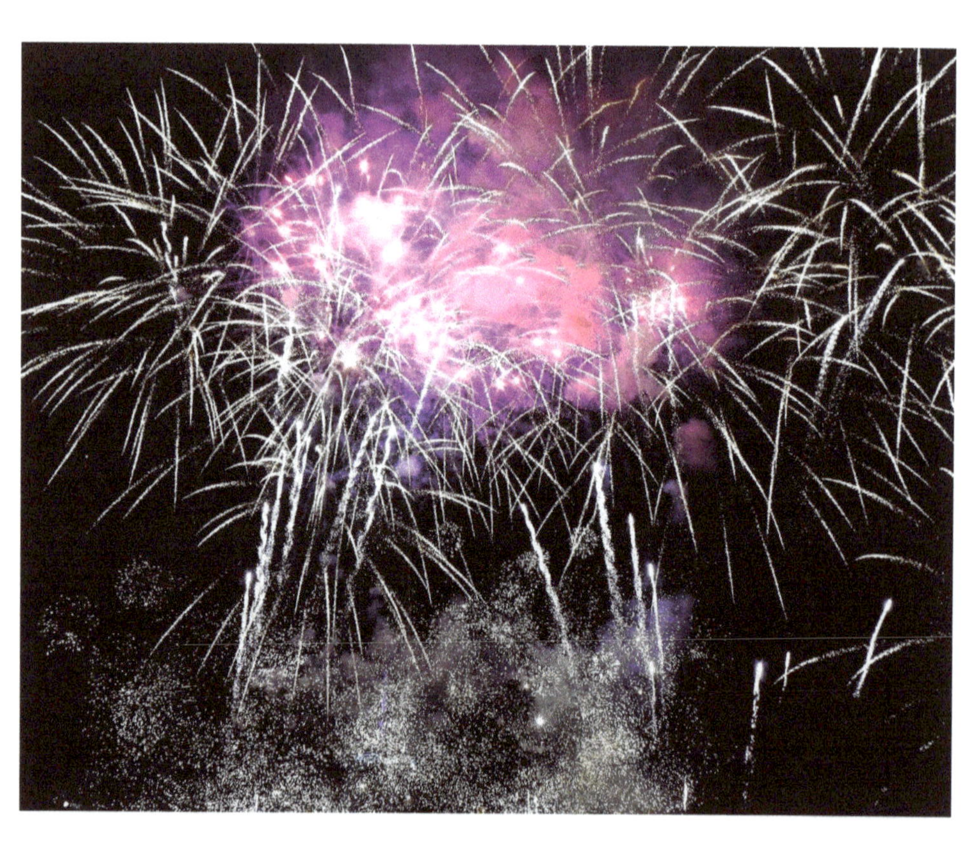

Fourth of July on the Clarion River

There was a time when the tradition was
anchoring in the cove, watching the town's fireworks display,
from boats crowded stem to stern,
while we drank and socialized our
way to the approaching darkness.
An event that was as traditional as
chilled strawberry pretzel salad on the Fourth of July.
Not this year.

Having drunks whiz fire flowers
across my bow while
listening to bro-country blaring
from a dozen opulant ski boats
with young dudes pissing off the bow,
old women flashing for floating beads, and
freaked out lap-dogs barking
through the flash-bangs, arid smoke, and
the bottle rockets' red glare,
exceeds what my
post-pandemic self can abide.

*I'm a Yankee Doodle Dandy*
*A Yankee Doodle do or die.*
Red-headed stepson of my Uncle Sam,
home on the Fourth of July.

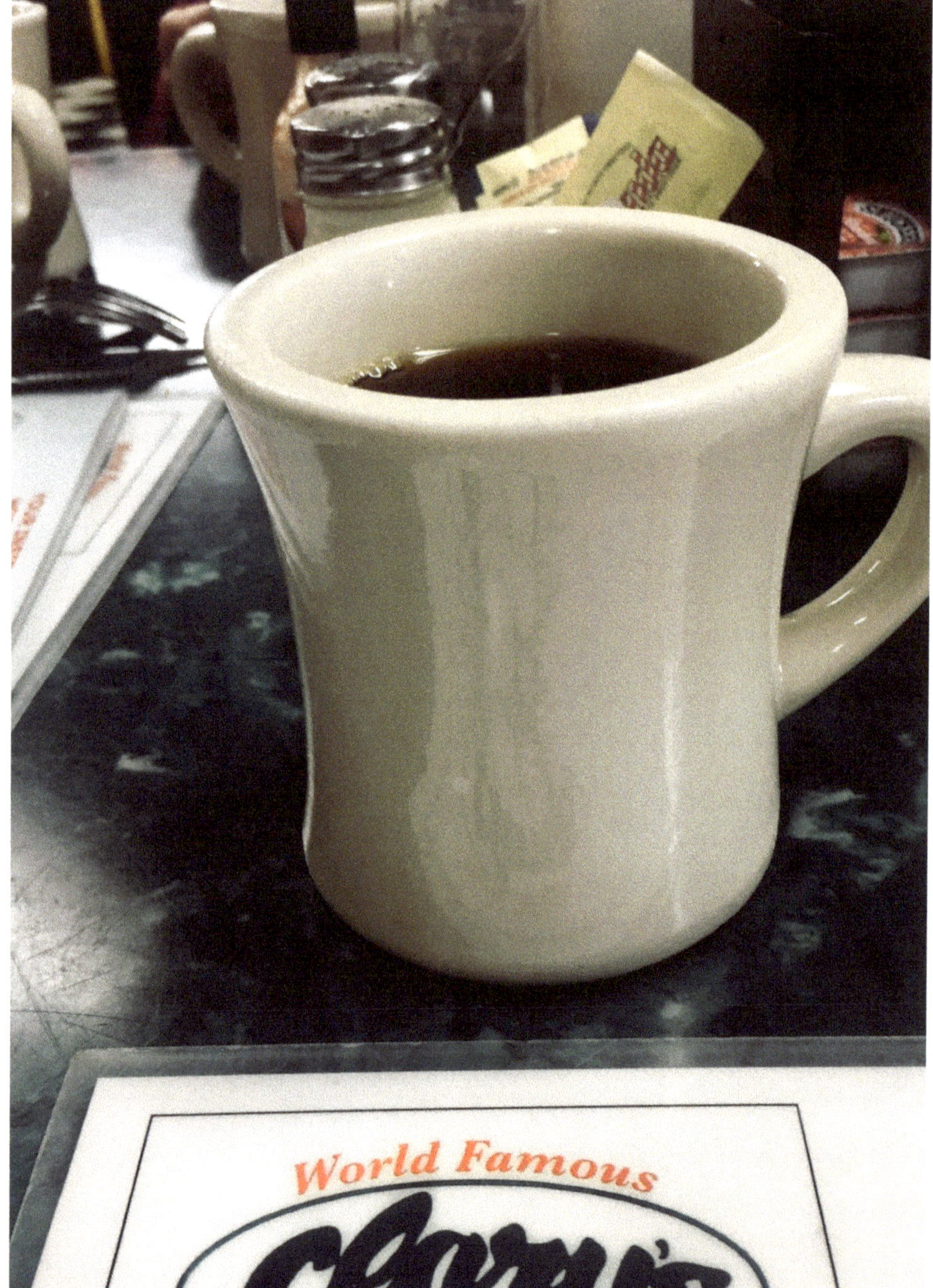
World Famous
clary's
CAFE

Black Coffee

During our final visit at the nursing home,
a few days before your
last large McDonald's coffee,
blonde with 3 sugars.
We laughed about
our scrapes and escapes.
Before you split for Florida
with these parting words:
*Free your ass and your mind will follow.*

You did a stretch in "juvie" earning
a reputation for quick fists, before
charming your way through 5 wives.
Now you've come home to die.
Deviant as ever, you jimmy
open the locked window to
toke on a banned vape pipe
smuggled in by some young nurse's aide.

In 1969, you were given the choice of
jail or the Army. You looked good in uniform.
I remember you going AWOL while on home leave.
Your self-described 10-day lust affair with an old girlfriend

Gibbo, the local constable, someone
with whom you had often butted heads,
found you hanging at Jake's Texaco station.

He took you to his house and fed you breakfast---
biscuits and gravy, country ham, fried apples.
When finished, Gibbo said,
*Let's just get this over with.*

He drove you to the county jail
where two MPs from Fort Hood were
waiting to take you back to Texas.
You had to pay for their plane tickets.

*Any regrets?* I asked.
*Yeah. I should have learned to drink my coffee black.*

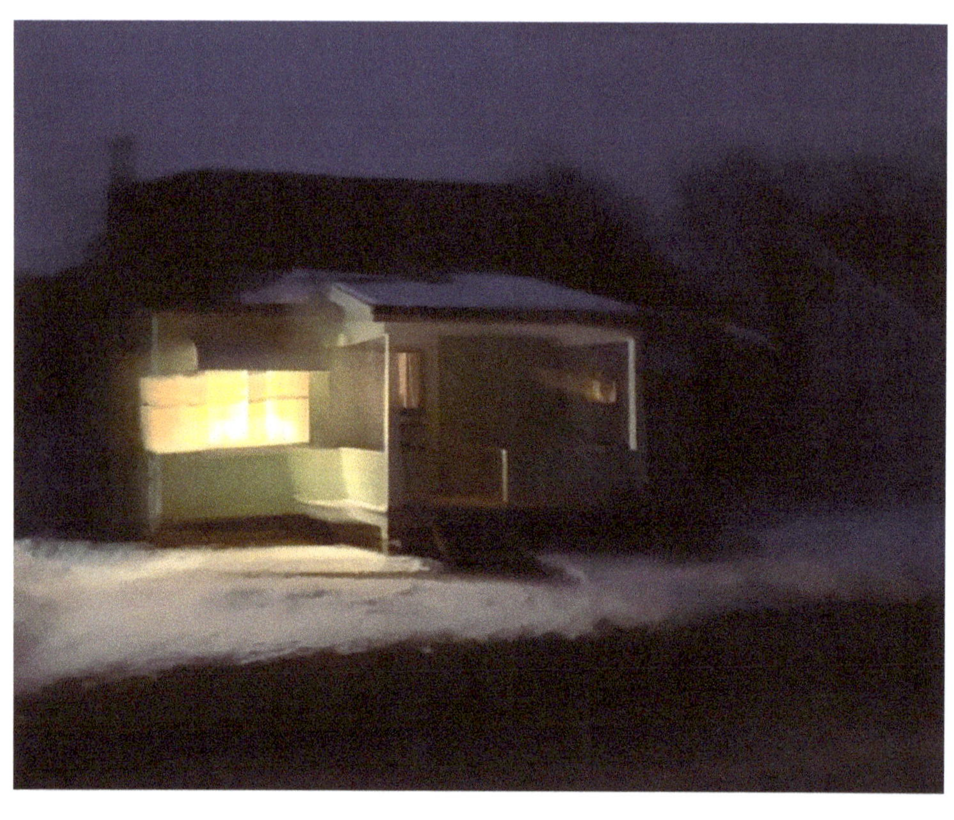

While Waiting to Change Worlds

My neighbor idles about the house.
Isolated, chemo sick, always fatigued,
avoiding mirrors, grieving her lost hair,
waiting for the end, which the doctor said
would be quick and painful.

Her husband hardly leaves his lounger.
Overwhelmed with sadness,
devastated with regret,
longing to make amends, but
knowing it is much too late.

Afternoons are filled with
a dull routine of westerns:
Gunsmoke, Bonanza, Maverick.
They sit together in grim silence
until, at last, she screams,

*If I hear one more gunshot,
I'm throwing that damn TV right out the window.*

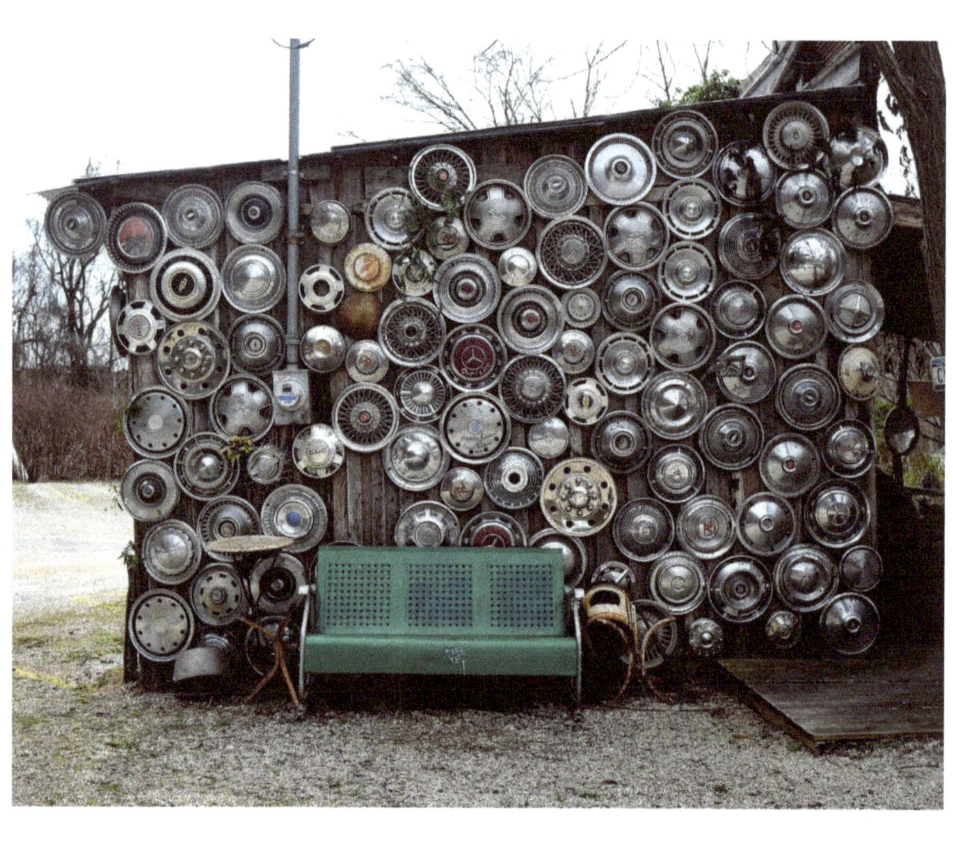

Check-out Line


I ducked into the Dollar Store
for some pop and Tums.
Scanning out ahead of me was an unmasked dude
who I recognized as a bartender I had
tangled with some 40 years ago.

I glanced at his purchases:
bag of chips, quart of milk, and
Bed Bug Killer.

Standing behind me was an unmasked woman
I drank beer and shot pool with 40 years ago
in the bartender's tavern.

I glimpsed her basket containing
lip balm, Mountain Dew, and
Preparation H.

I was masked-up with dark glasses
under a camo hoodie---my pandemic look.
They failed to recognize me.

I am standing between a guy who once threatened to kick my ass
and a woman who ran her fingers through my hair.
On the same night in the same bar.

I thought of the serendipity of our 40-year reunion.
Him with bed bugs. Her with hemorrhoids.
Me with my Little Debbies

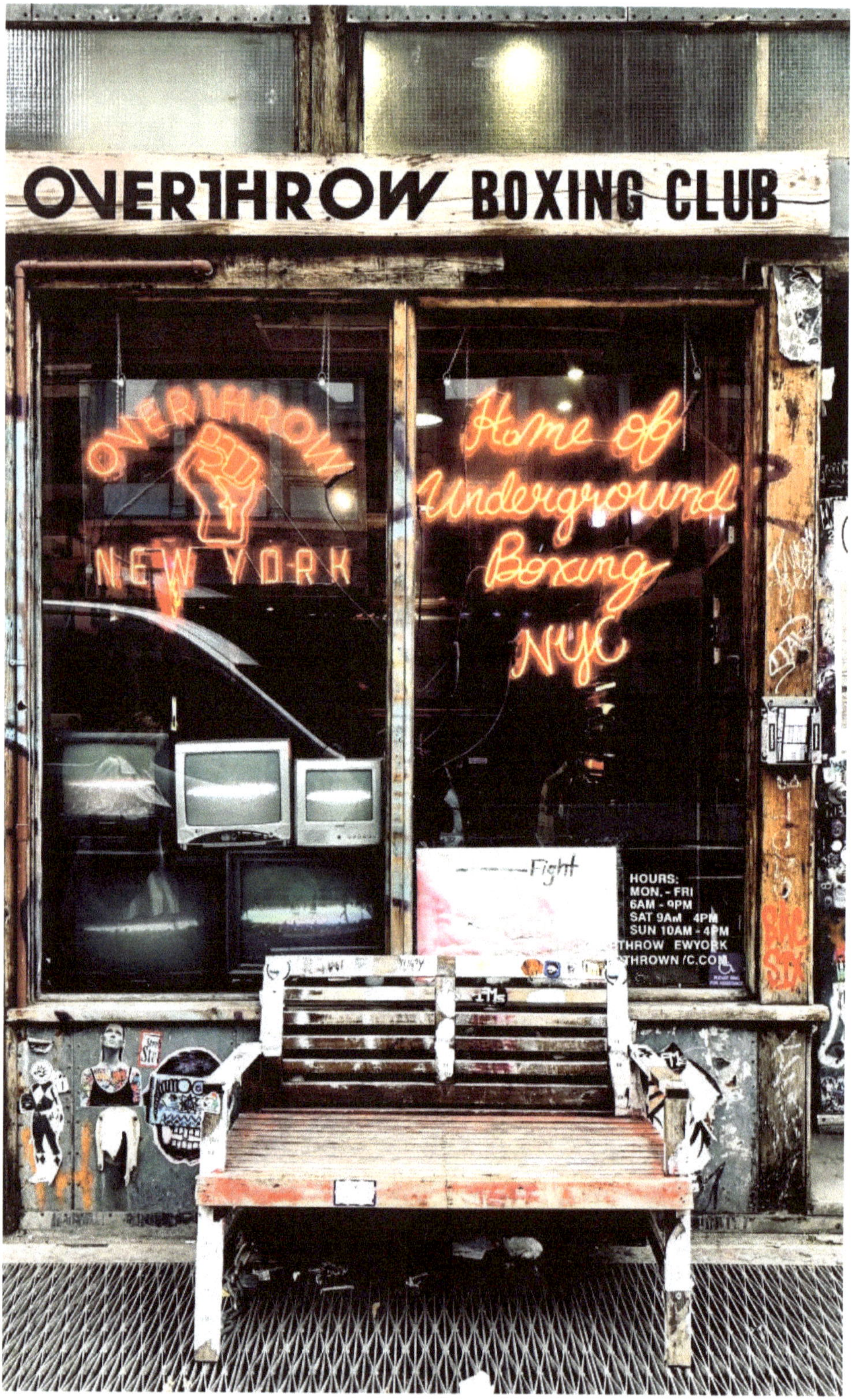

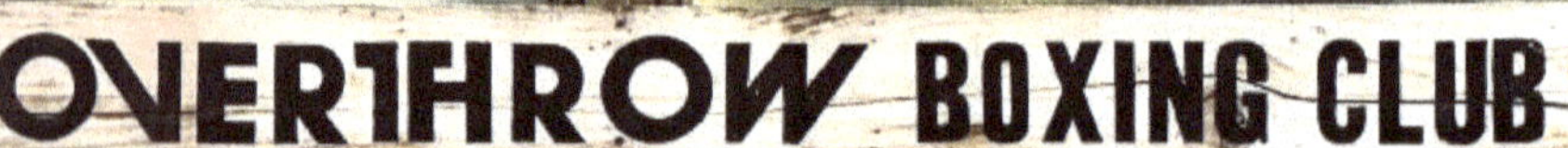
OVERTHROW BOXING CLUB

OVERTHROW
NEW YORK
Home of
Underground
Boxing
NYC
Fight
HOURS:
MON. - FRI
6AM - 9PM
SAT 9AM 4PM
SUN 10AM - 4PM
THROW EWYORK
THROWN /C.COM

Iron Mike

Mike Tyson
enters:
no robe,
no socks,
no ring-walk music,
black trunks,
black shoes,
white hand towel
cut to fit his head,
stone cold tattooed face.
Furious mayhem arrives
with this warning:
*Everyone has a plan
until he gets hit in the mouth.*

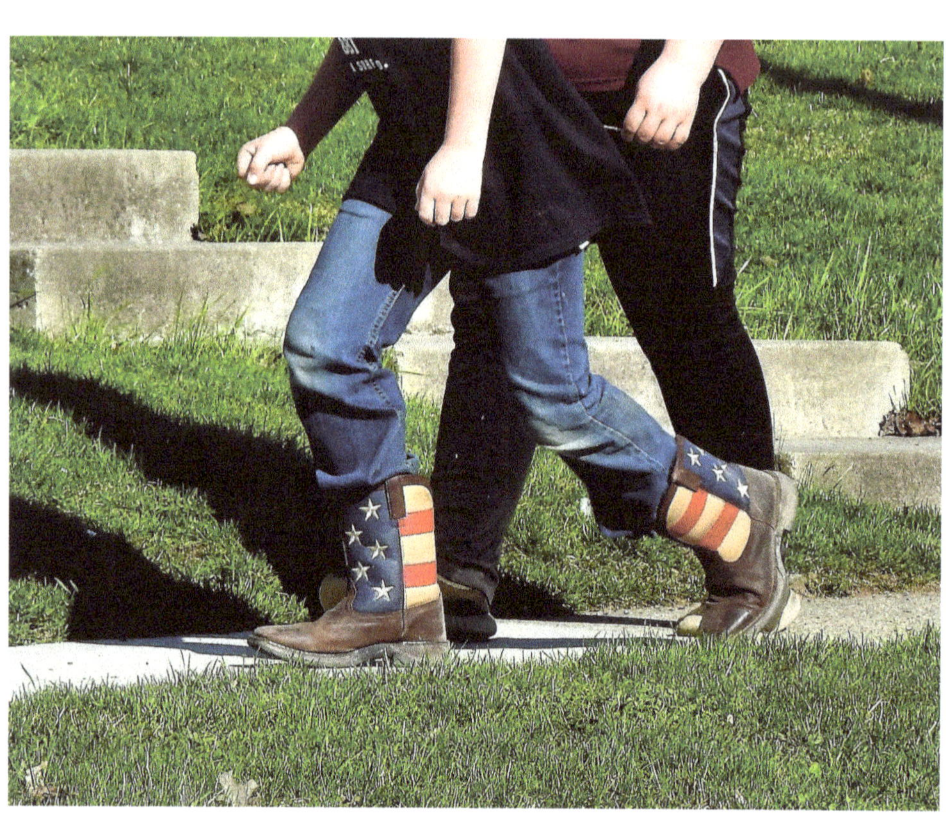

Lessons from My 3rd Grade Teacher

Miss Floyd taught me
how to be still and
listen to the geese flying south
in early September.

*That will be you one day,* she said,
with a squeeze on my shoulder.
It was years before I understood
what she meant.

Miss Floyd showed me where to look
for wild raspberries before the orioles ate them,
how to deadhead the flowering zinnias,
whispering that we were
tricking them into making
more blooms, as if
she didn't want them to know.

Miss Floyd read
*Robinson Crusoe* to us.
I still recall my goose bumps
when Crusoe found a human
footprint in the sand.

Cannibals!

She read us *The Jack Tales,*
yarns from the hills of home.
and introduced books by
her friend, Jesse Stuart, whose
*The Beatinest Boy,*
I read it over, and over.
She wanted us to be proud of
our emerging sense of place.

Miss Floyd was named
"West Virginia Teacher of the Year" in 1968
and spent that time visiting all 55 counties,
sharing her experiences, insights, and wisdom.
She taught for 45 years at
the same elementary school.
She advised the 4-H Club and supervised

the summer recreation program,
where she always wore flowing dresses
with snow white tennis shoes,
and regularly beat us at ping pong.
She led us on field trips to museums,
Camden Amusement Park, and
the Coca-Cola bottling plant.
I would rather have been with her
than eat when I was hungry.

Forty years passed before our
paths crossed again at a flea market.
She immediately recognized me and
called out my name. We shared memories and
laughter before she told my wife
what a sweet boy and good student I had been.
Miss Floyd remembered and praised
all of her former students that same way.

Before parting, I thanked her for what she had done for me
and so many other kids in our little community.
I thanked her for accepting me,
a struggling kid from the head of Turkey Creek,
growing up in a house with no
running water and a coal-fueled
pot-belly, Buckeye stove for heat.
I thanked her for driving up that muddy,
rutted holler in the middle of winter
with my school work when sickness
nearly caused me to repeat the 3rd grade.

I thanked her for
rejecting my self-doubts,
never consenting to my shame,
kindling my childhood dreams, and
seeing in me what was hidden from myself.

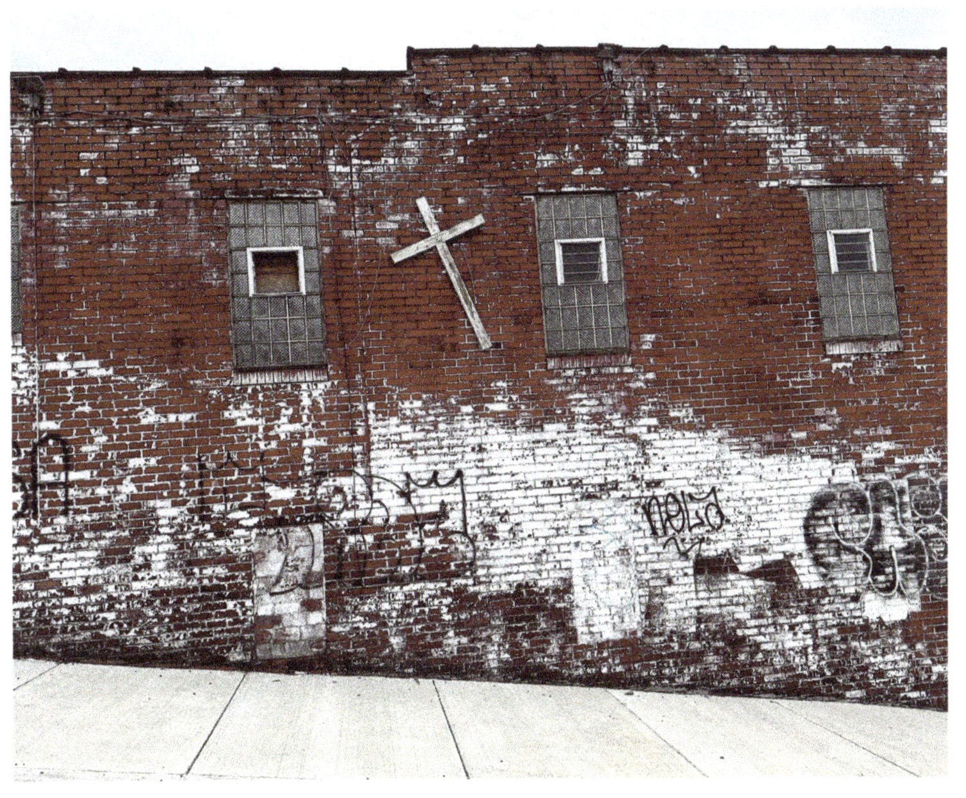

Existential Angst of a 5-Year-Old

I once asked my Mamaw
where God came from.
She quickly pinched by ear with,
*You're not to supposed to
ask those kinds of questions,*

Is it easier to believe
than to question?
Is it more satisfying.
to always have an answer
than not having one?

We can't 'believe' truth into existence.
Yet, The Truth eternally abides,
supremely indifferent,
unchanged.

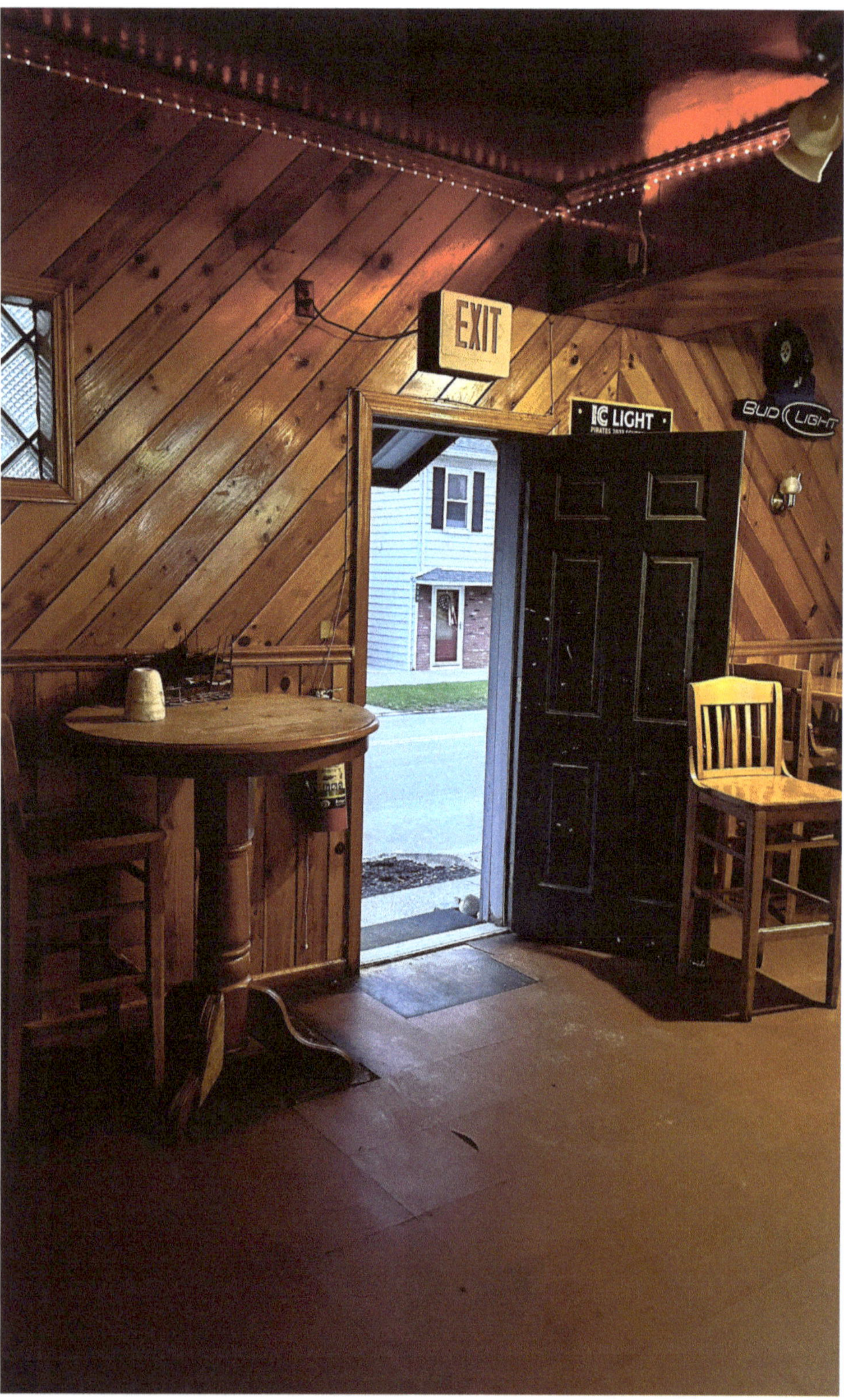
EXIT
IC LIGHT
PIRATES
BUD LIGHT

Soaps and Ice

Day-drinking at
a little beer joint
in a dusky, pinched, Pittsburgh neighborhood.
Just me and the Momala bartender
silently watching a soap opera
on the tiniest TV ever made.

A beautiful small-screen coquette
mixes an Old-Fashioned for
an unexpected handsome guest
in the perfect TV den.
My barkeep leans over and mutters:
*You know--- they always have ice on these shows.*

She's right.
No ice trays pulled from a freezer.
No hasty runs to the Quik-Stop.
A brimming ice bucket always at ready.
Perfect cubes dropped into an impeccable glass.
Pour, stir, sip.

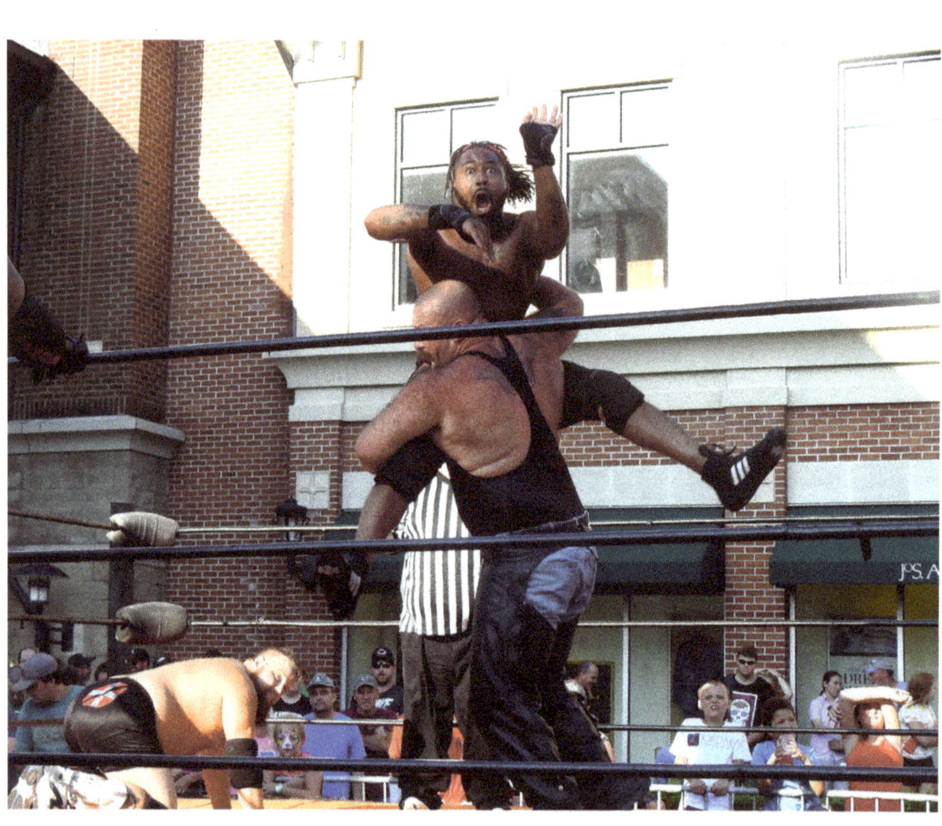

He Won't Ever Be Gone

He and his daddy
attended Studio Wrestling
matches every week and
bought Marvel comics.
He later ran their pool hall

while praising the
Avengers, Jeet Kune Do, and Hulk Hogan,
selling beer for carry-out only.
Unless he knew you.

I knew he had been sick.
In hospice.
Where he died yesterday,
two days before his 69th birthday.

The newspaper death notice said:
There are to be no services at this time.

I hope he is in some unknown paradise,
talking up Bruno Sammartino,
browsing Spider-Man #1, and
trading one-inch-punches
with Bruce Lee.

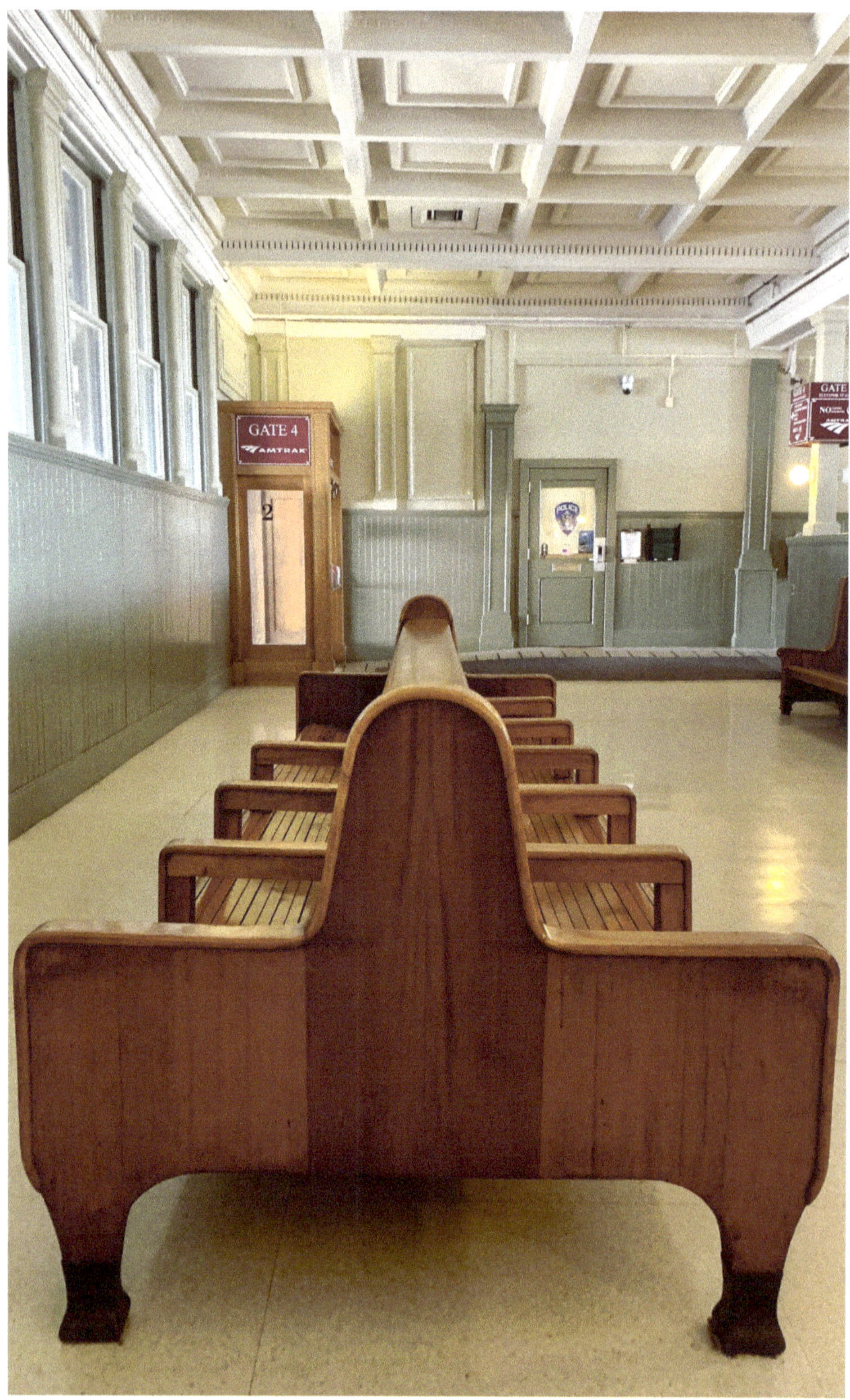

Learning to Wait

Not waiting is hard.
Waiting is harder.
Sometime soon,
in a while,
before long,
aren't measured by clocks,
but with tenacity,
patience, and
grit.

Waiting is an art.
Each moment a
lesson in patience,
a gentle reminder
that life's most beautiful
journeys unfold
in their own time,
weaving threads
of anticipation into
the fabric of our existence.

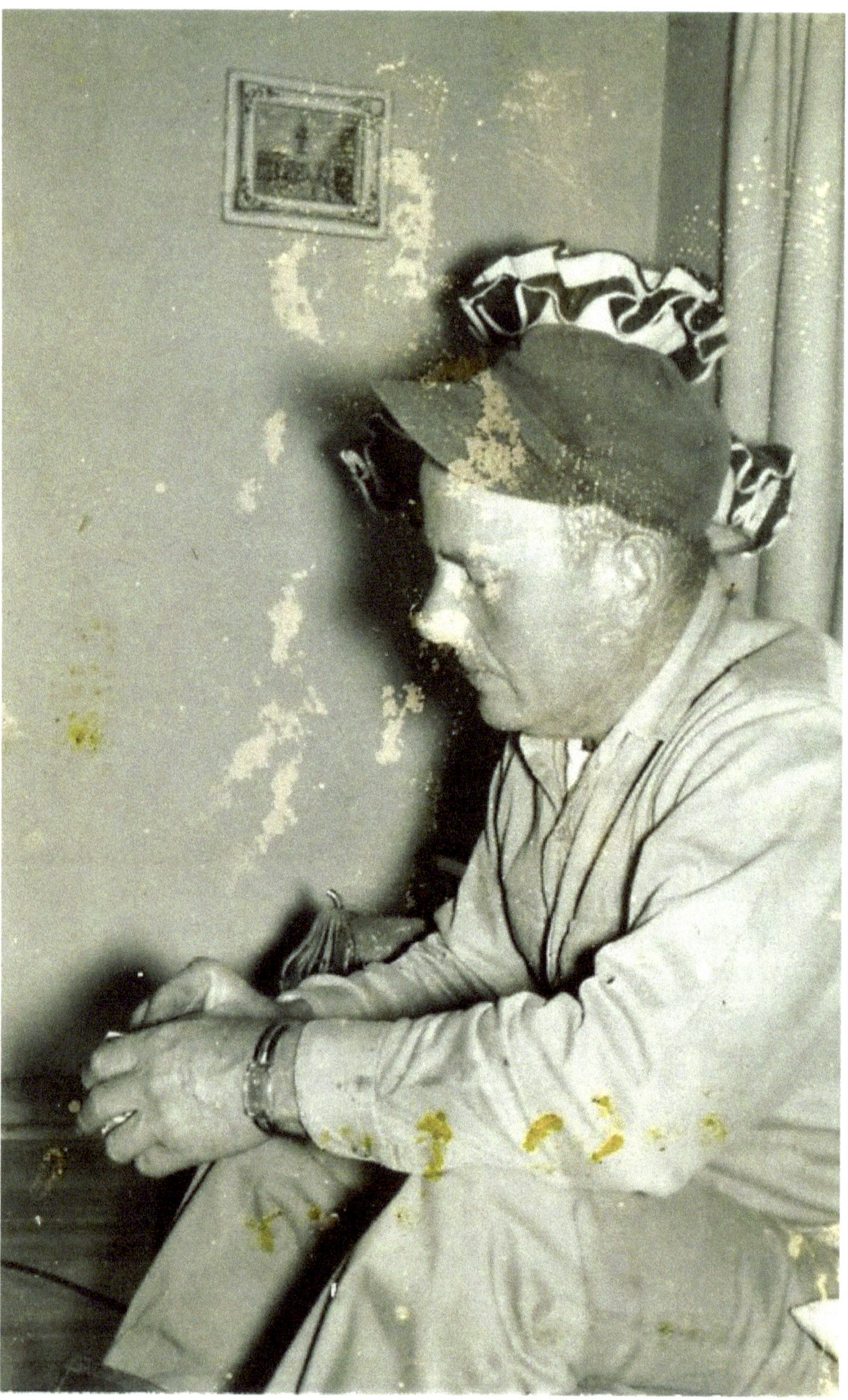

Uncle Wilmer: A Debt to the Devil

My great-uncle Wilmer Clary
took me in when I was 8-years-old.
He would say to me,
*You get used to it,* when the
water in my nightstand glass froze overnight.

At day's end, I'd watch him sink
into his old, worn easy chair,
chain-smoke Camels and drink instant coffee.

Wilmer was one of eight Clary kids
raised on a dark, steep hillside farm
up Goose Run, West Virginia.

His wife, my great-aunt Frankie, a saint,
once told me, *He wasn't raised,
he was jerked up by the ears.*

Wilmer and two of his brothers
married three Nance sisters from
over on Turkey Creek.

Their father, Pop Nance, used to say:
*The Devil owed me a debt
and paid me back in Clarys.*

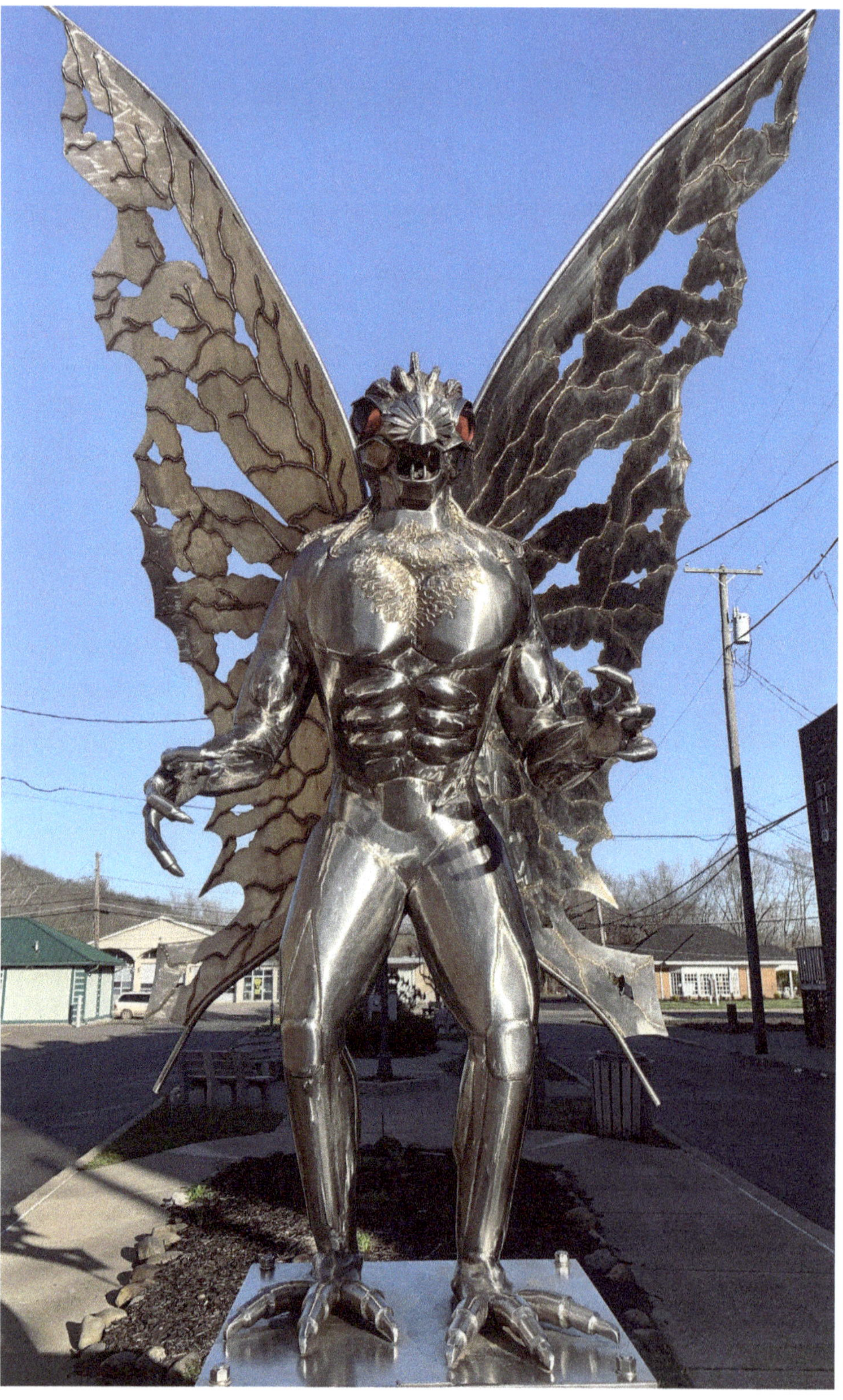

Texting With my College Roommate after 40 years

Tony: *The Bible says we have to bless each other so we can live in love. So, I'm sending you this message.*
*Today is a day of blessing! I bless you. Your heart. Your health. Your home. Your life. In the name of Jesus.*

Me: *You going to church now?*

Tony: *Yes, I do go to church. Don't you go?*

Me: *No*

Tony: *I will pray for you*

Me: *Good. I need the prayer and you need the practice.*

Tony: *Bless you! Do you believe in anything?*

Me: *It's all a mystery to me. I know I don't go for that fundamentalism stuff I was raised on. You still indulge?*

Tony: *I drink a beer or two.*

Me: *Ok. You still burn one?*

Tony: *Sometimes*

Me: *Ok. Sounds like you aren't a fundamentalist, either.*

Tony: *Oh, I forgot. You're a Democrat*

Me: *And you're not. I should have known back when you were ordering all of those Brandy Alexanders. Do you believe in science?*

Tony: *I believe in the Son, the Father, and the Holy Ghost*

Me: *Ok. But, do you believe in science?*

Tony: *No!*

Me: *What do you do when you are sick? Do you take any meds? How are you communicating with me right now without science?*

Tony: *I believe that Jesus died on the cross for your sins and mine. Do you believe in that?*

Me: *Ok. Does that mean you can't believe in science?*

Tony: *Some of it. But, I believe in Jesus. Don't you?*

Me: *Some of it*

Tony: *There you go!*

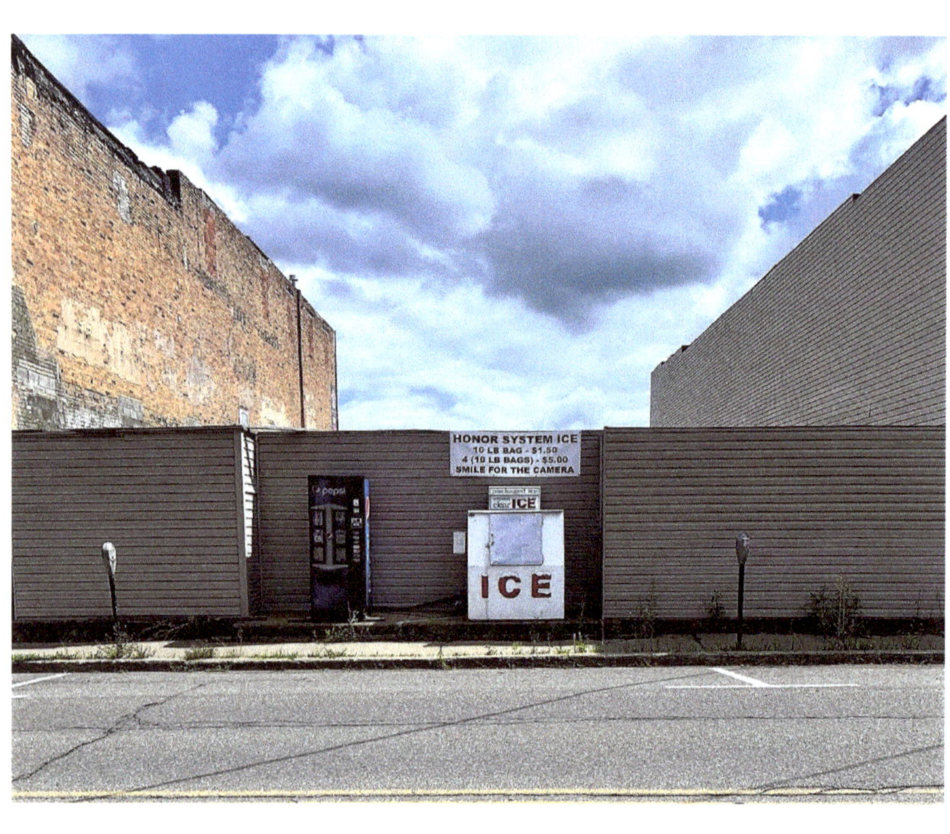

HONOR SYSTEM ICE
10 LB BAG - $1.50
4 (10 LB BAGS) - $5.00
SMILE FOR THE CAMERA
pre-bagged ice
clear ICE
ICE
pepsi

Online Dating

Several once-married friends are single again.
Hurt, lonely, seeking connection,
they have gone online hoping for renewal.

I ask Charlie how the search is going.
He says he was invited to a pool party
and told to bring refreshments.

When he arrived, everyone was naked.
*So what did you do?* I inquired.

He shrugged with, *Grabbed my Pepsi and went home.*

My buddy Denver says he met a woman online
who likes to go out dancing.
He told her he was willing but wasn't much on his feet.

They went out two-stepping at a cowboy bar,
but Denver confessed, with a snicker,
*I looked like a bobber in rough water.*

He insisted on hearing what I thought,
but the best I could say was:

*If they're interested, you'll know.*
*If they're not, you'll be confused.*
*Take your time.*

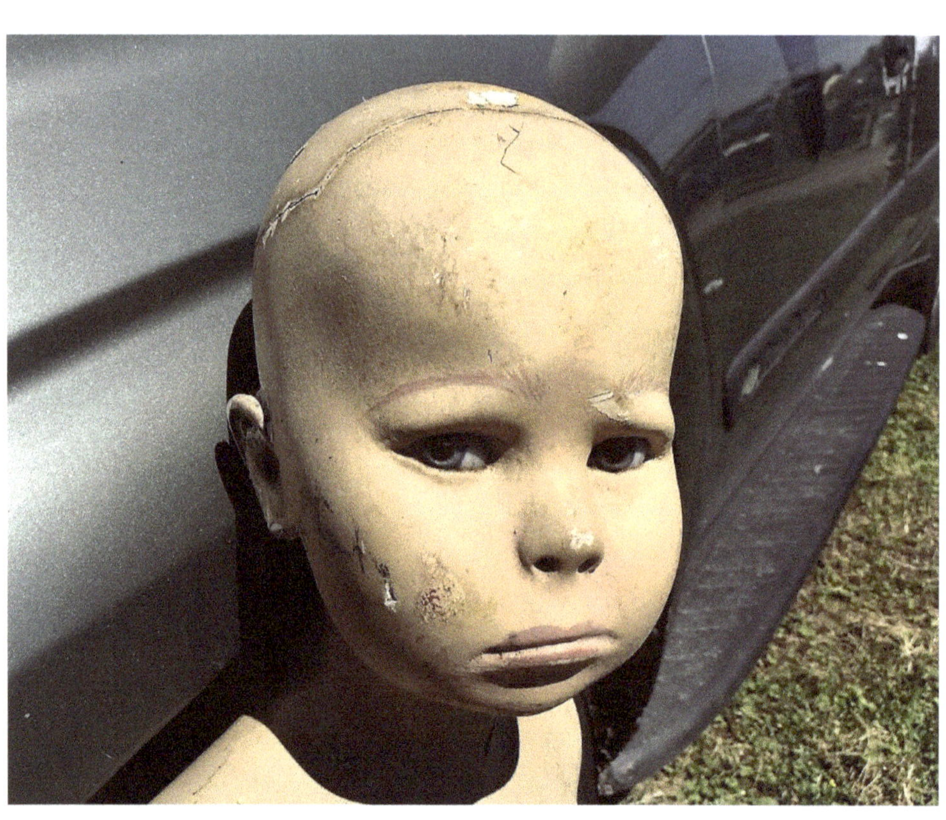

Conundrum

What do you say when
the toughest guy you know,
Chalk Eye,
cries at your kitchen table?

Offer an encouraging word?
An arm around the shoulder?
A drink of whiskey?
No advice. Lord, no advice.

Then like a swift, black cloud
uncovering the moon,
the moment passes.
Grim gives way to grin.

*Remember the time when we*
*rolled my old Corvair*
*and walked home in the snow*
*to your Mamaw's house?*

*I sure do, Chalk Eye,*
*tell it again.*

This is how ends and beginnings
end and begin.

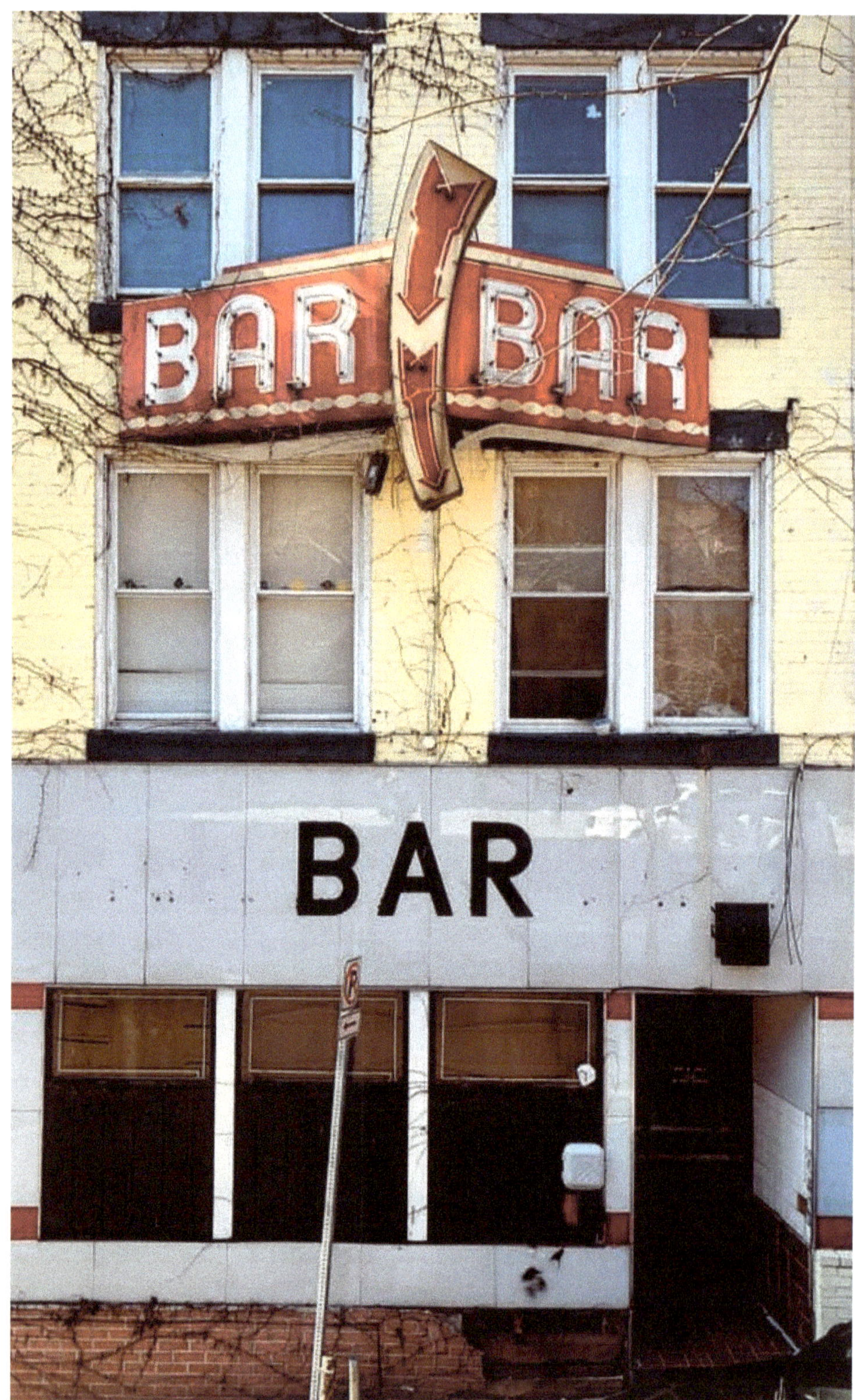
BAR
BAR
BAR

Saying Hello to an Old Goodbye

She spotted me
before I saw her with
that Cheshire Cat grin,
whiskey in hand, moving close
in her casual sashay.

*Boy, if you'd 'a just stayed home*
*we might'a had a chance.*
*But you had a troubled heart.*
*other things to do.*

I did and I did.
She was hard to quit with
her glad eyes. Her truth.
Her cathead biscuits.

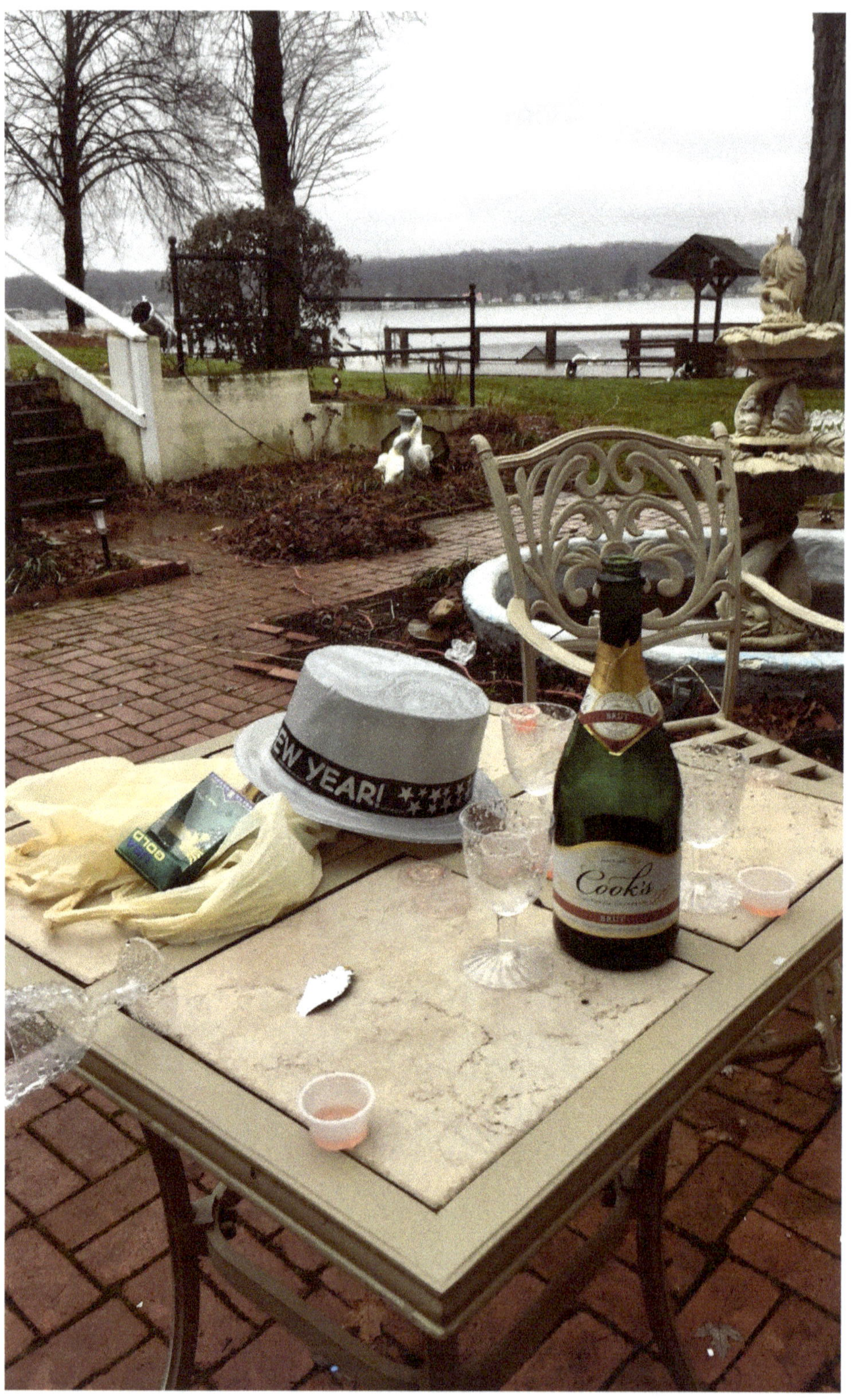
EW YEAR!
GOLD
Cook's
BRUT

How to Host a Good Party

No canned beer, bottles only.
Wine is red, whiskey is Irish.
No food until the end.
More people than chairs.
No devices, no pictures.
Dancing is good, conga lines are not.
Always invite a controversial woman, one
who is confident, decisive, resilient,
who generates debate, defuses boundaries,
acts on unconventional views,
tolerates difference,
and provokes conversation that
pierces the evening air like
flaming arrows.

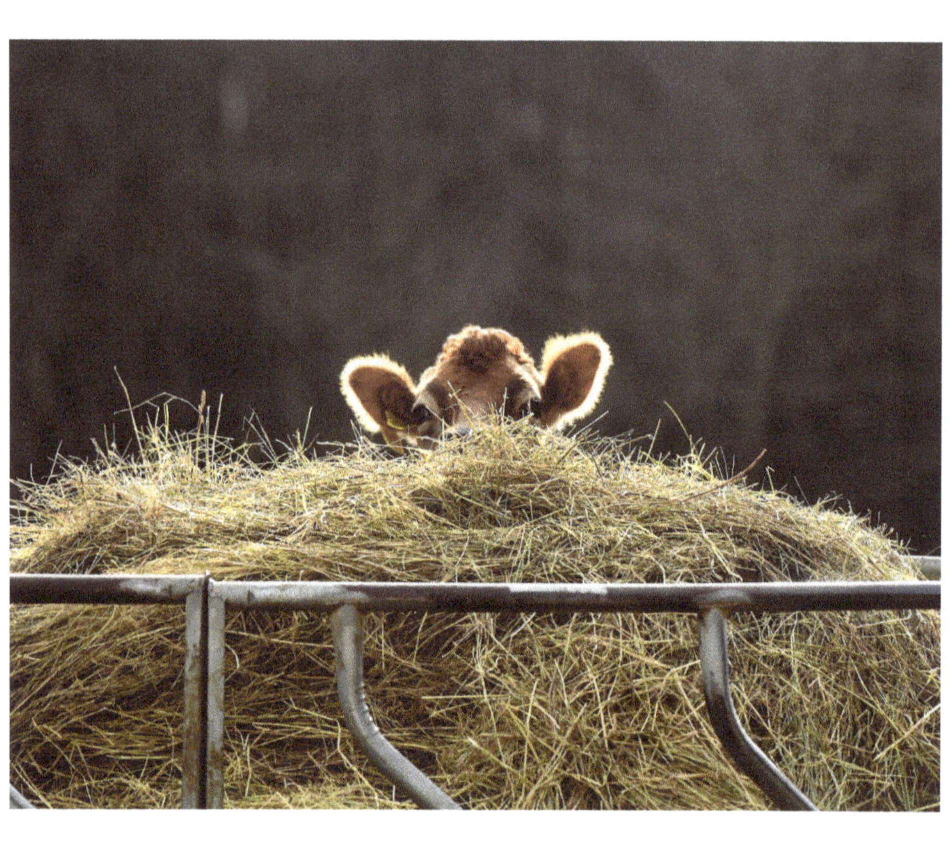

A Good Day

Today, I learned about
Tariffs, borderless puzzles, braided streams,
and the Witchcraft Act of 1735.


I saw a hungry hairy woodpecker tapping suet,
a marsh hawk swooping up an unsuspecting vole,
and a bearded dragon flicking a pet store cricket.


I heard the shriek of a bald eagle on the wing,
the screech of brakes from a speeding coal truck,
and Muddy Waters screaming out *Mannish Boy.*


I felt the cold, mesmerizing, Clarion River,
the shock of black mud up to my knees,
and the bliss of a long, thriftless, hot shower.


I whiffed pinto beans and ham cooking in an iron kettle,
the pungent scent of wet plantation pines,
and an abandoned peppermint patty wedged in the truck.


Today, I was reminded to
*Never let a day go by.*

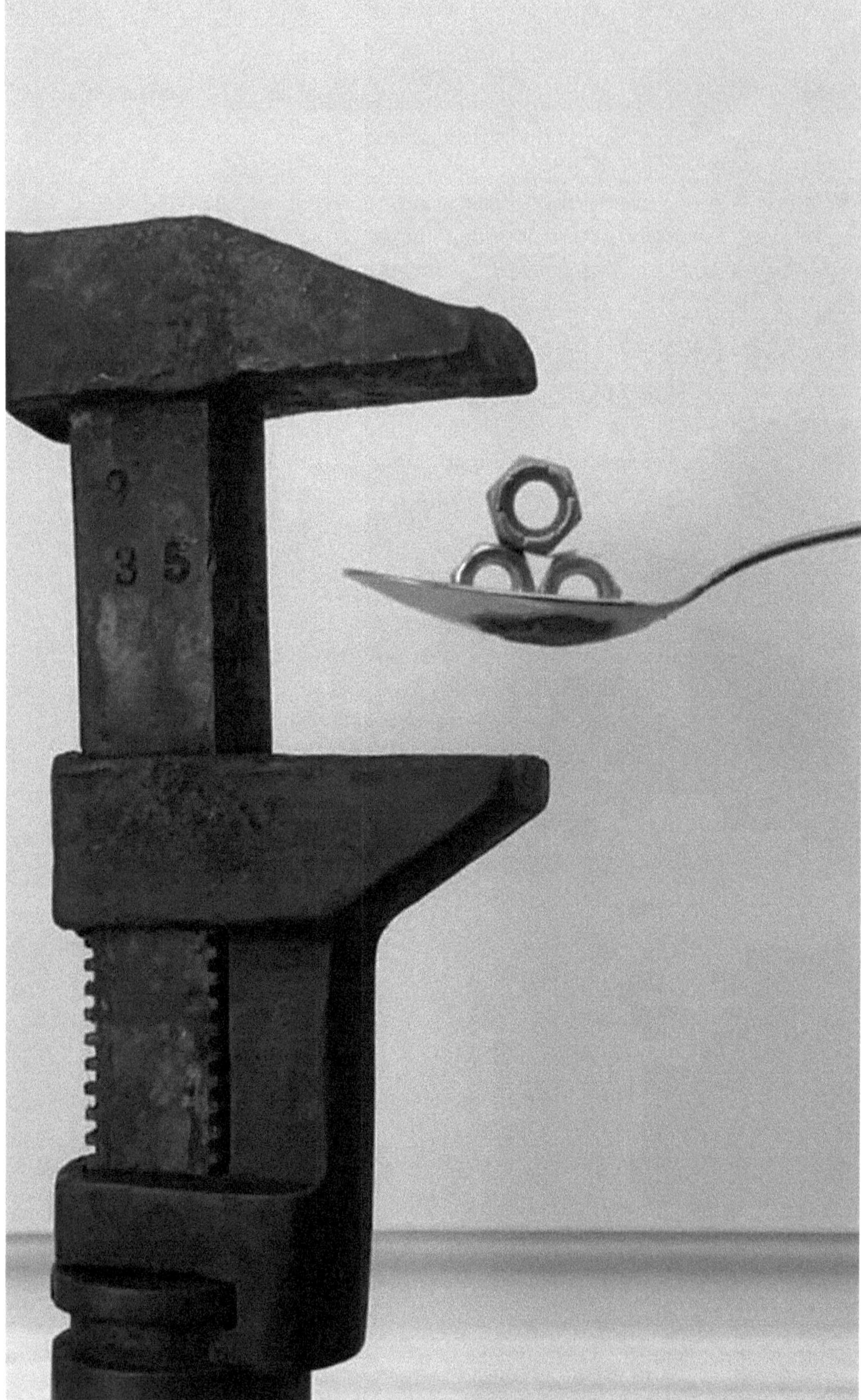

37 Things I like

1.Reading bumper stickers in the Walmart parking lot.
2. How I feel after my 2nd cup of coffee
3. People with grit
4. Little Debbie Zebra Cakes
5. Friday nights with no alarm for Saturday morning
7. Retirement---letting go without stopping
8. People who can ease into a conversation without taking it over
9. Zambelli fireworks on a hot Pittsburgh summer night.
10. Late August night sounds of distant thunder and crickets chirping.
11. Bare November days while stump-sitting in the woods
12. Oyster dressing with a plump Thanksgiving turkey
13. The Stillers
14. Ireland--where people look like me
15. Old dogs napping with kittens
16. Homegrown fried green tomatoes
17. Afternoon naps on a rainy day
18. 2 fingers of Jameson over 1 cube of ice
19. Laughing with old friends, sharing memories
20. Songwriters who can make you cry then make you laugh
21. Bamboo sheets
22. Walking right into an empty chair at the barber shop
23. Clicking unsubscribe
24. Locating a gobbler on his roost at daylight.
25. Hearing my grandson say,"Pop"
26. Deep, dark hollers where whispers fill the air
27. Black Guinness from the tap and white lies along the bar.
28. Having the tractor fire up after sitting all winter
29. Jerry Jeff on the truck radio in the pre-dawn darkness
30. Opening a much-anticipated email that begins with: "It gives me great plea-
sure..."
31. People who can deliver a great story
32. The Jerry Garcia Band's version of Sugaree
33. PNC Park
34. Cathead biscuits and gravy
35. Peepers hollering in the spring
36. A Pilot Precise V5 fine point pen in black, when a keyboard just won't do.
37. Leisurely foot rubs from my darling wife.

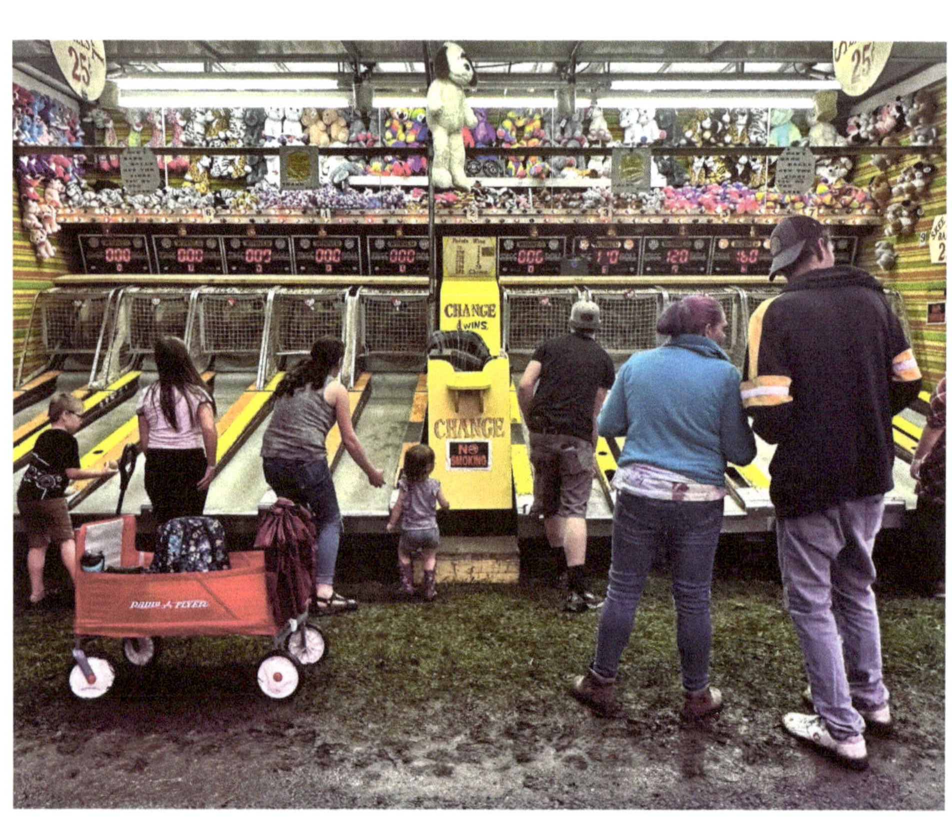

25¢
25¢
CHANGE
WINS.
CHANGE
NO SMOKING
RADIO FLYER

Skills

Chain saw starts but won't run.
I head for help at Earlie's garage,
filled with bars, sprockets, orphan chains.
The pungent odor of gas, grease, and oil.

*Your carb seals need replaced,* Earlie says.
*I'll call you when it's ready*

Crossbow cocked but won't fire.
A visit to the Archery Shack,
crammed with bows, broad-heads, stabilizers, the
acrid smell of fox urine and "doe in heat".

A kid, still in high school, explains,
*This only happens when it's cocked
to the dry fire position.*

Loose braces on my
grandfather's bent-hickory rocker.
Off to an old friend's cabinet shop
filled with lathes, planers, clamps,
the aroma of freshly milled cedar.

*The dowels have worked loose from the joints.
An easy fix.*

I thought, easy fix? Then
replied with a laugh,
*So, where was I when you learned all this?*

He pauses, lowers his square, and says,
*You were out shooting pool at The Joker.
I was scraping my knuckles at Brady's Hardware.
Things worked out for both of us.*

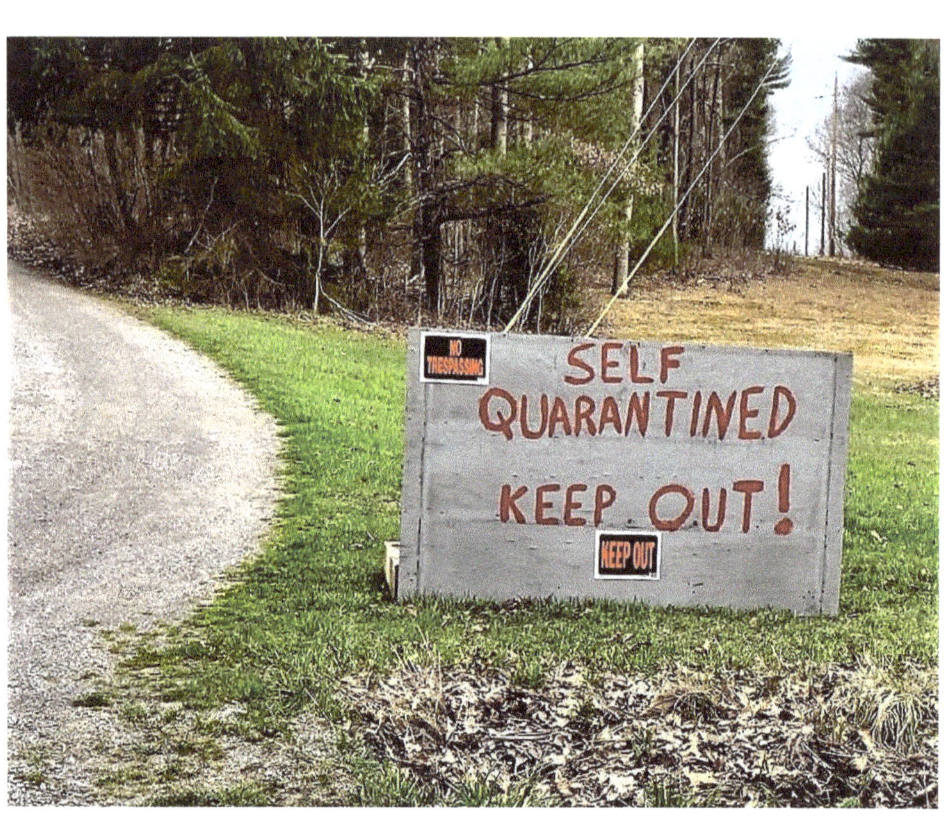
NO
TRESPASSING
SELF
QUARANTINED
KEEP OUT!
KEEP OUT

Time of the Varse

Carl Jung claimed that the masses
breed psychic plagues.
Billy Graham preached that
a contagion of *Easy Believing*
faces the church.
Wallace Stevens believed thoughts are an infection
with some becoming an epidemic.

*Siri* identified these as
our current societal epidemics:
Depression, AIDS, human trafficking,
obesity, racism, gun violence,
opiate use, suicide, dementia,

And now a pandemic has arrived.
A global scourge
that threatens all of humanity
in every region of the world.
It seemed inconceivable.

My wife and I now swap new words:
Asymptomatic, ventilator, codon sequence,
epidemiology, pathogen, vector-borne,
super-spreader, pre-exposure prophylaxis.

We practice new behaviors:
Self-isolate, shelter-in-place,
remote work, masking-up,
zooming, doom scrolling,
flattening the curve.

We speculate about tomorrow, and
the day after tomorrow, and
the day after that.
Hoping for relief.

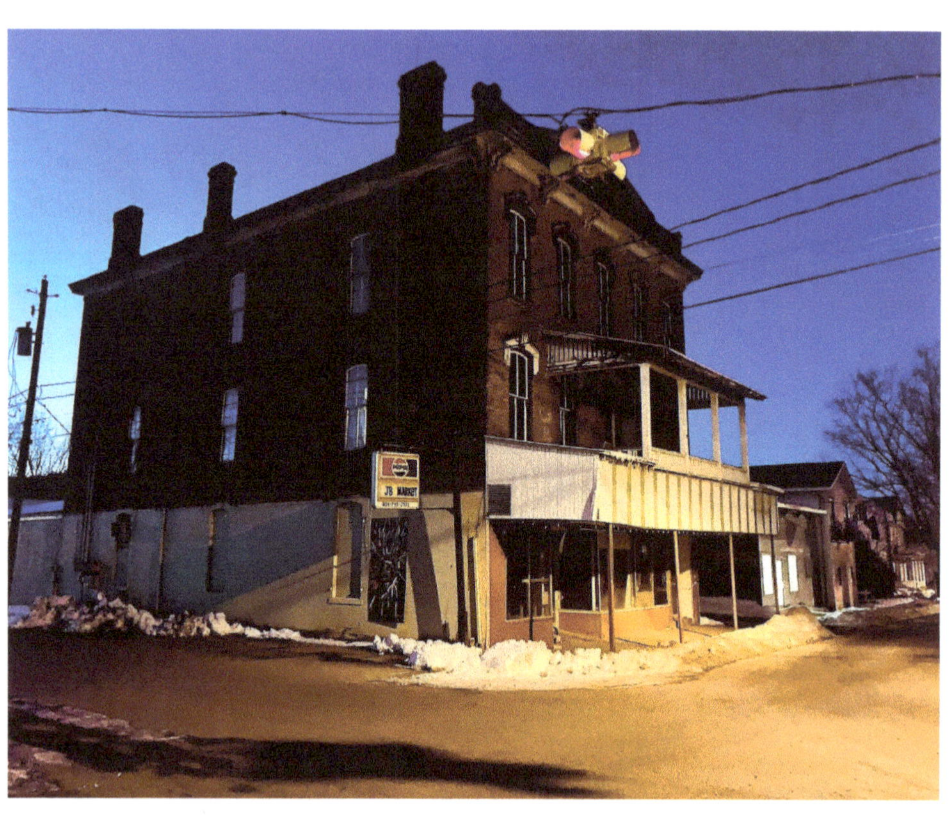

Pepsi
JB MARKET

Fortuity

A life-long smoker
blows out the candles on
her 90th birthday cake.

A scientist friend of mine
often tells me that
unexpected surprises are
to be expected.
Incongruity Theory, he calls it.

A menopausal grandmother
asks her husband to start
planning their gender reveal party.

An aging coal miner
steps into a little West Virginia
mountain top general store
and asks:
*How are the lobsters today?*

Snow in summer's heat,
a red leaf on green branches,
laughter in a tearful eye,
truth in paradox.

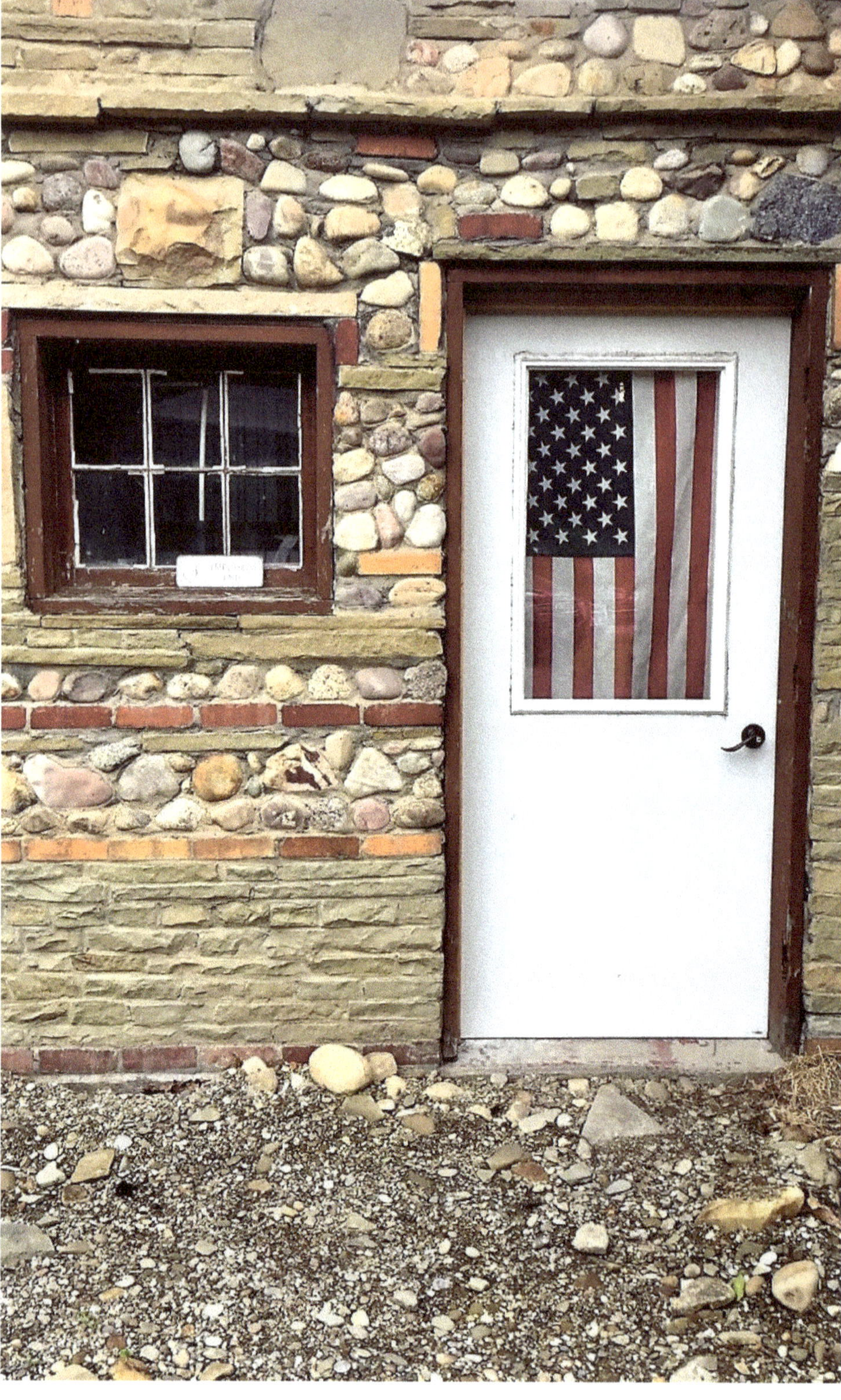

24 Hours

While riding my thumb to Florida
in the summer of 1974,
a 30ish woman from Detroit,
picked me up just south of Cincinnati.
She was heading for a solo camping trip
to the Smoky Mountains.
After a couple hundred miles,
we decided to camp at
a Tennesee state park.

Her traveling gear included a
Kodak XL 55 Super 8
movie camera that we aimed
at typical touristy targets:
worn trails, jutting rocks, our camp,
each other.

Later, around the fire,
I filmed an interview with her.
She was a secretary, still with her parents,
desiring to become self-reliant and daring.
This road trip was her big first step.

The next morning,
she drove me back to
Interstate 75 and we parted.
She ran the camera as
I waved goodbye, and
climbed into the back of
a sour apple green Falcon Ranchero.
And that was it.

No addresses written on scraps of paper.
No phone numbers exchanged.
No last names offered.
She would now be in her late 70s.
Does the film still exist?
Did she gain her independence?
Did she lead a happy life?
Is she still living?
Does she remember?

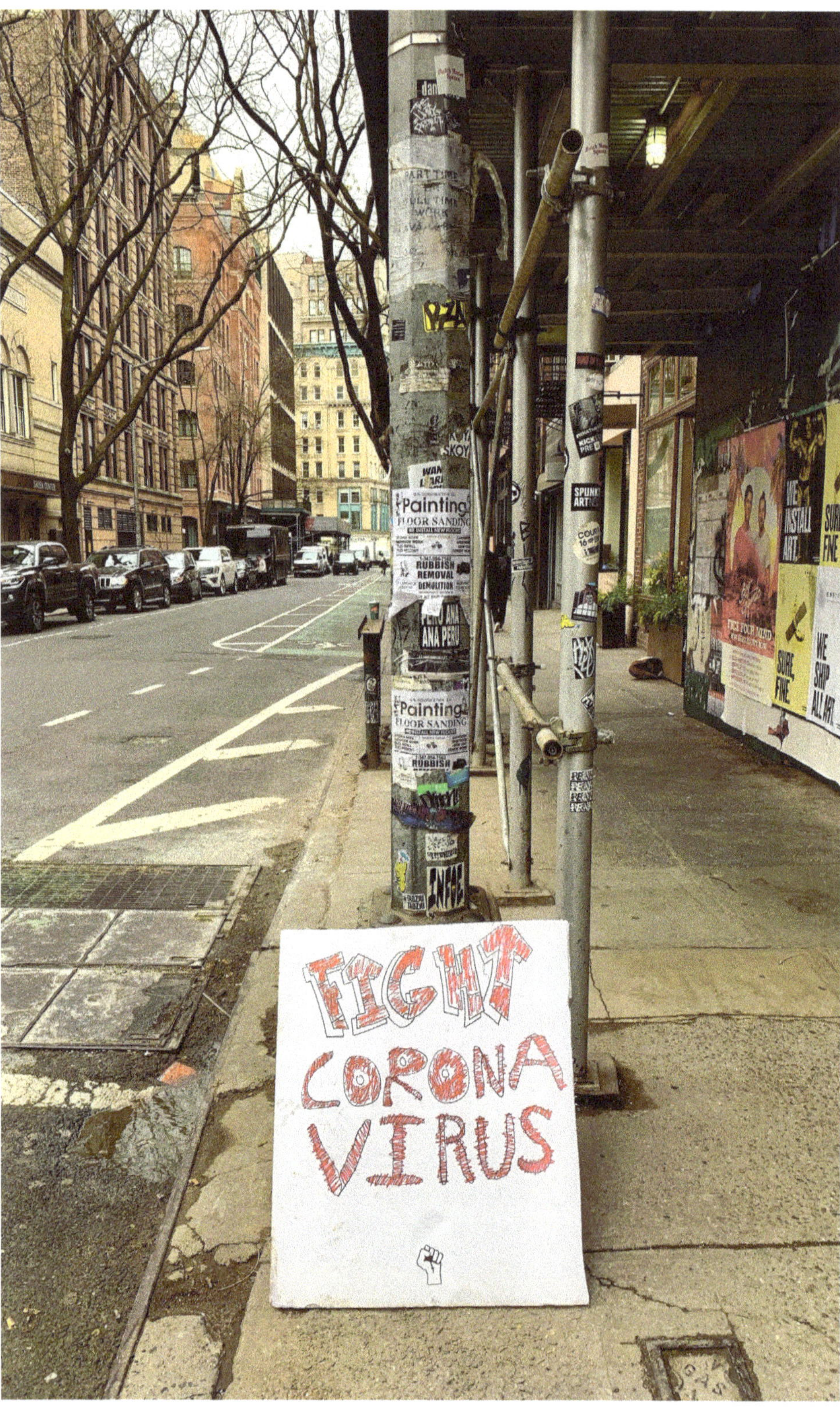

FIGHT
CORONA
VIRUS

Today Was a Good Day

On the first day of
The second impeachment of
Donald J Trump,
I received Covid vax #1
and celebrated with
gratitude and thanks
by eating Chinese take-out
off the hood of my pick-up truck
in the parking lot of a strip mall
on a frigid, snowy,
northwestern Pennsylvania afternoon.
It was a good day.

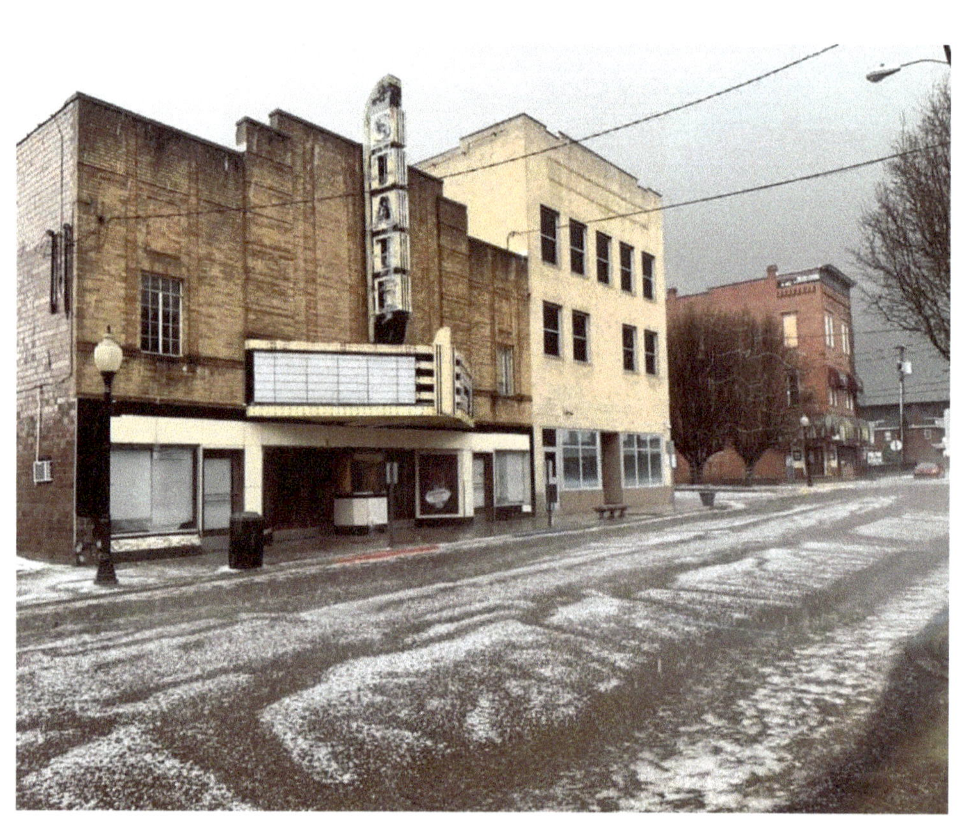

STATE

Back to the Steel City Lounge

Today marks two years
since I last sat on
a barstool in a real bar.
No frozen blended drinks.
No drinks with cute names.

I step into the thick, blue, miasma,
where second hand smoke as a carcinogen
is never a topic for discussion.
At the door, a 5 foot high
Yosemite Sam says:
Varmints must be this tall to be served.

I grab a stool in the center of
the U -shaped bar where
a dozen regulars, all over 55,
in Red Man caps and Steeler hoodies
are talking, laughing, and leaning
over Iron City long necks.

*There ain't nothing sexier on a woman than French nails*

    *I hate Daylight Savings Time. Made-up by golfing politicians.*

*Sometimes you just have to try it a few times to know it's wrong.*

    *I was in the 3rd grade before I realized that no one else got up at 4:00 and
went to school smelling like cow shit.*

*We don't hate each other like the news wants us to believe,
    but some people deserve to be hated.*

A wise writer friend of mine
once told me our lives are our own,
but filled with other people's stories.
This afternoon, for a little while,
strangers tolerated my interest in theirs.

I finished my beer. Paid my tab. Left a tip.
I walked out into the cold of my
second socially isolated pandemic winter,
feeling enlivened by the chatter and
curious about French Nails.

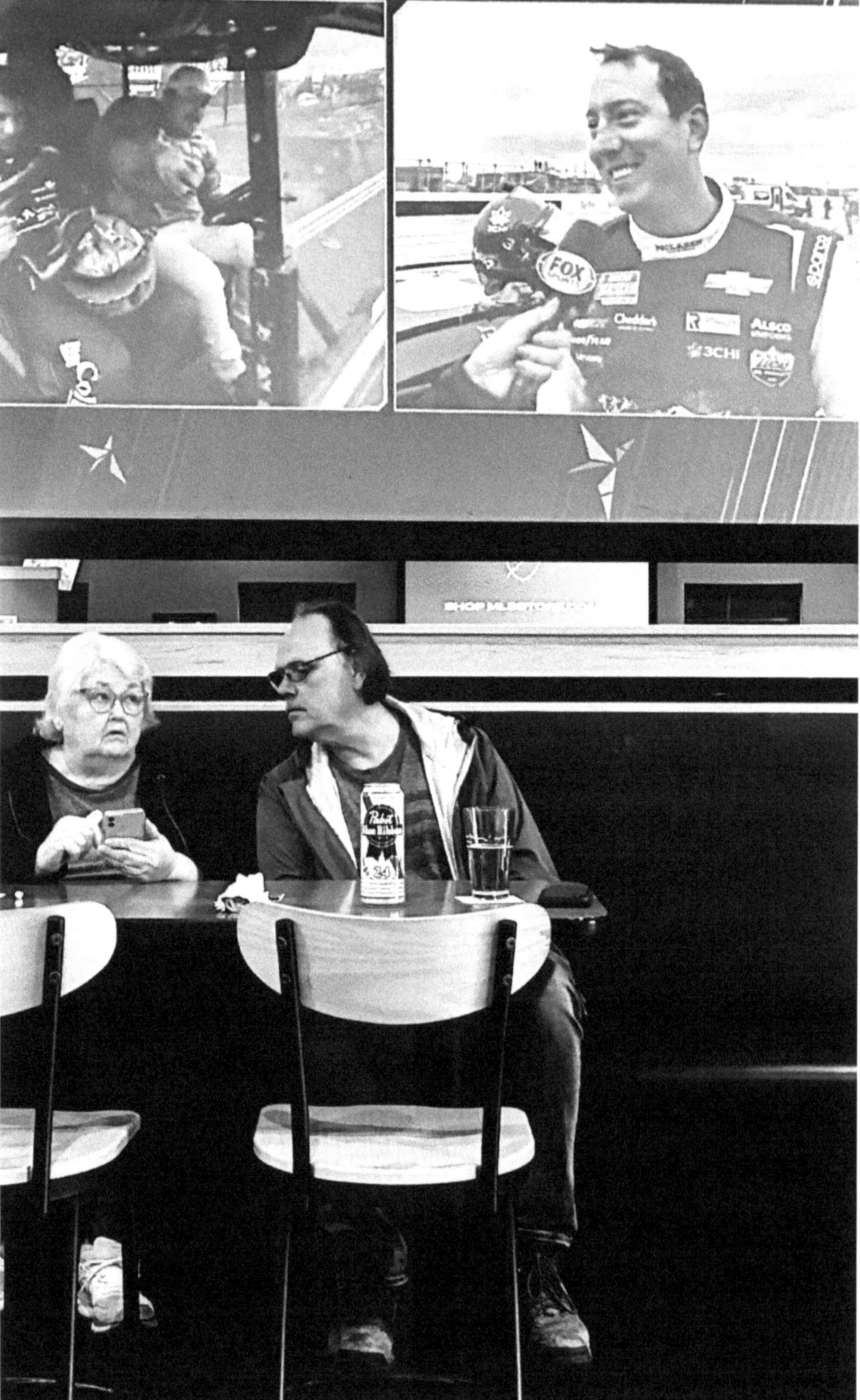

Who is Virgil Tate?

Home in West Virginia, sitting on the cabin porch,
I asked my neighbor:

*Do you know Virgil Tate?*

Sure, he grinned. *He grew up over on Dummy Holler,
up past the snake handling church. He
used to be on the volunteer fire department.*

*His mom and dad are Anzel and Faye.
His sister is Ramona. She bought
Bill Miller's place up on the old road.*

*He used to be bad to drink,
but he got saved and
now leads a pretty good life.
Why? Do you know him?*

*Kind of,* I replied.
*He once broke a beer bottle over my head.*

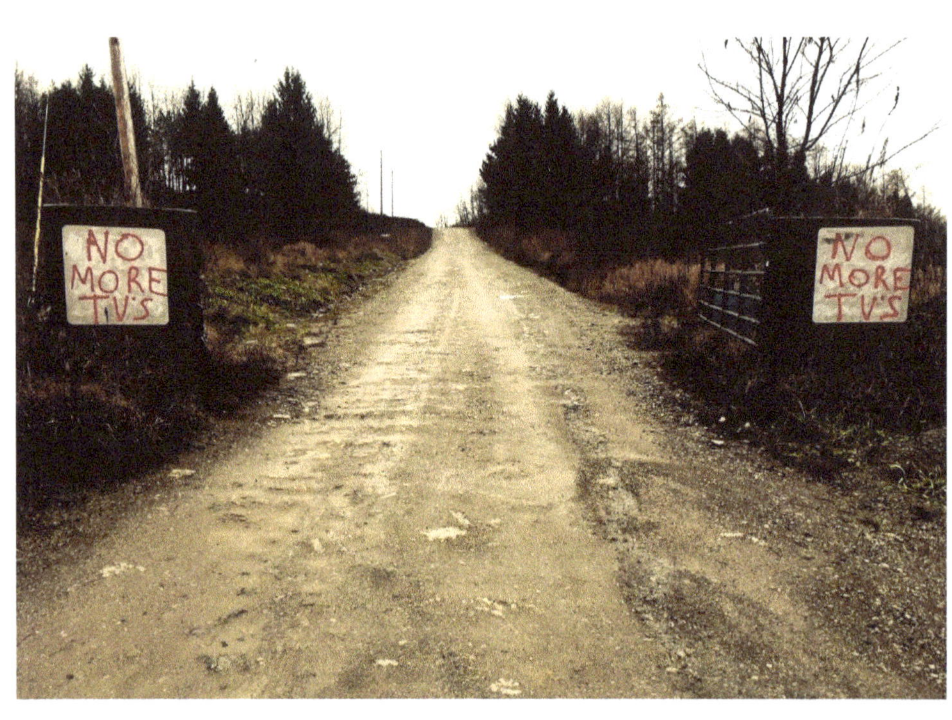
NO
MORE
TV'S

NO
MORE
TV'S

Black Friday

The Big Box Store had a
Big Sale on big screen TVs.
A nervous, but eager, sales clerk,
Timmy, quickly appeared.

Information regarding OLED, HDR, and resolution
was offered for the 20 TVs
simultaneously broadcasting the
same vibrant jungle birds program.

*This model is great for sports.*
*This is the preferred one for movies.*
*This smart unit is perfect for wifi streaming.*
*What kind of shows do you like to watch?* he asked.

A good sales pitch must be succinct.
It must offer solutions to perceived needs.

*I like to watch porn, Timmy.*
*What do you recommend?*

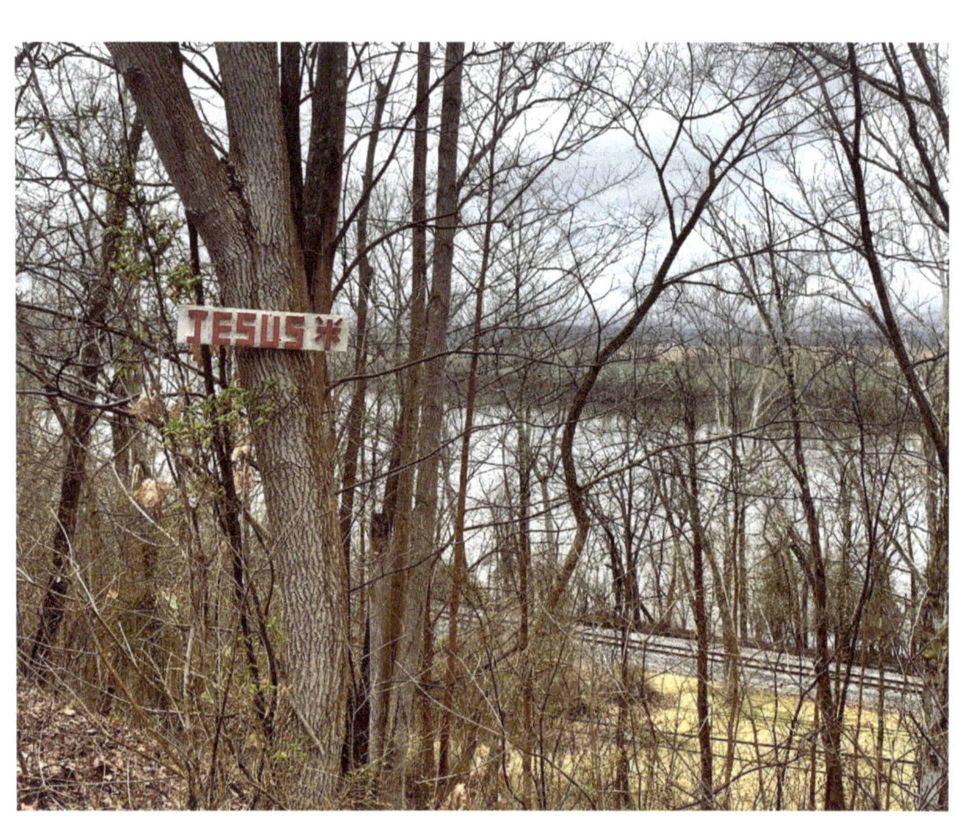
JESUS *

Remembrance

After seven decades, the dead
become as important to me as the living.

I think of them often.
I hear their voices in my mind:

Burrhead telling me, *You did alright for yourself
in spite of being kicked from curb to lamp post.*

Great-aunt Jessie's final words to me:
*I'm not afraid. I have no fear. I want to reach my
heavenly home.*

My last farewell with cousin Kenny, when
he gave me a firm handshake and we locked eyes.
I told him I loved him and said,
*I'll see you again sometime.*

He answered, *Yes. You be careful.*
And then he smiled.

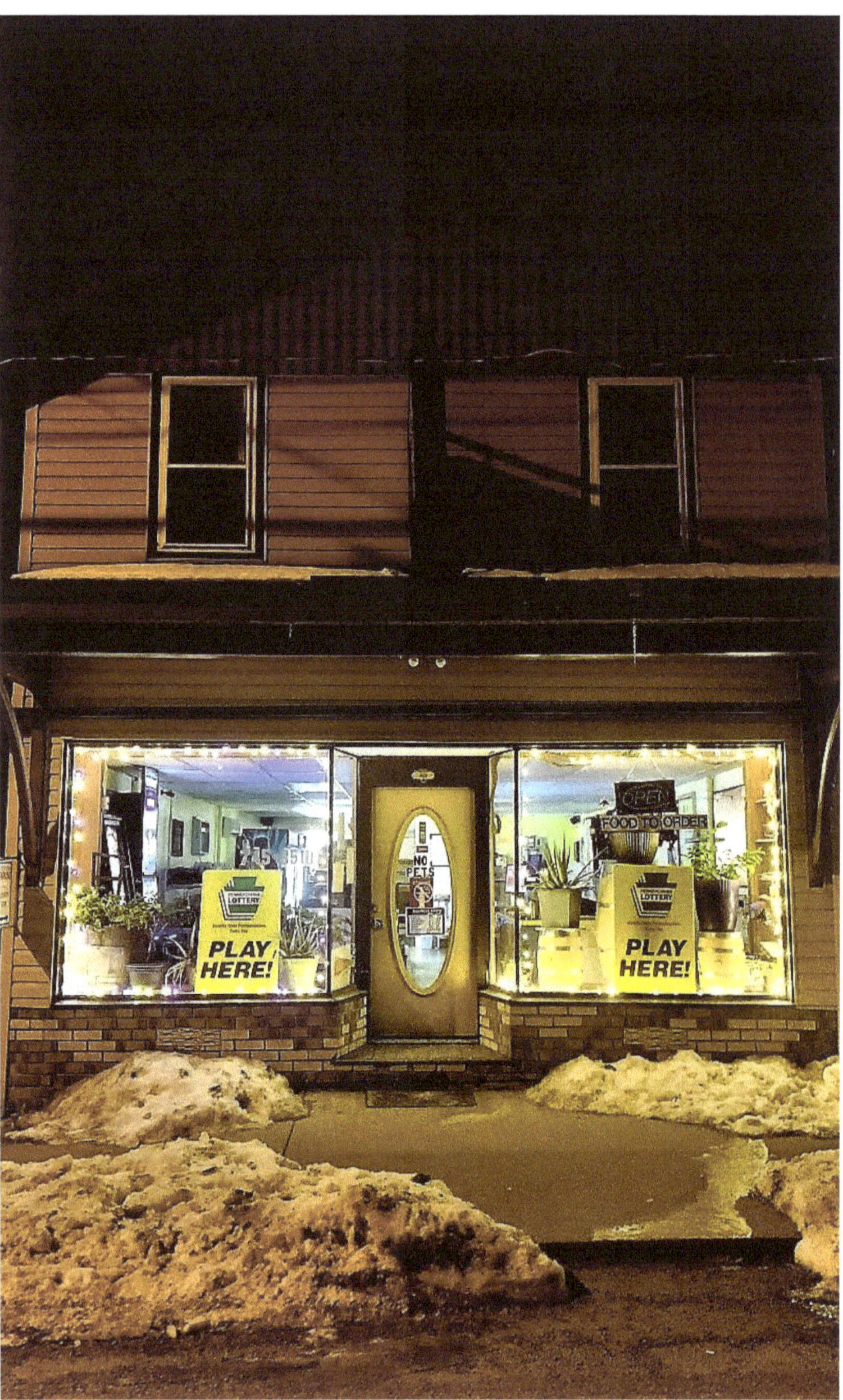

PENNSYLVANIA LOTTERY
PLAY HERE!
OPEN
FOOD TO ORDER
NO PETS
PENNSYLVANIA LOTTERY
PLAY HERE!

Lunch at the Korner Restaurant

It is the kind of place
where men dip their fries in mayo
and debate the wisdom of swapping out a
universal joint while using an adaptor kit.

> *The garage is so busy, my dog is answering the phone.*
> *Charlie---how you been? No one sees your face anymore.*

> *Alright, I guess, except I'm stiff where I used to be limber*
> *and limber where I used to be stiff.*

Two 30-something men from the machine shop across the road
stop in for rhubarb pie and ice cream.

> *Listen, if you can't fix it, you gotta learn to stand it.*

> *I know, I know, but I don't want to lose her.*

In the rear booth, a deep sigh is
followed by a raspy, cigarette voice:

> *Backhoes and laptops have been my whole morning.*
> *What neck-tied engineer dreamed that one up?*

Snippets of chatter emerge from neighboring tables:

> *The Stillers need to cut loose from Big Ben. He's done.*
> *Past his prime, 300 lbs, bad elbow, pouts too much.*

> *Hey, you're confusing him with Bradshaw.*

> *No, Ben has better hair.*

I sit here listening with nowhere to join in.
Universal joint repair? I know nothing.
What about universal health care, or the universe?
How did it begin? How will it end?

Relationship break-up? I've had a few, but
am no authority on advice giving
What about discussing fate versus free will?
How can we lose what we don't possess?

I could comment on the perils of aging,
the frustration of uncooperative laptops,
the Steelers, Pens, and Pirates.
But, I don't. I just ask for the check.

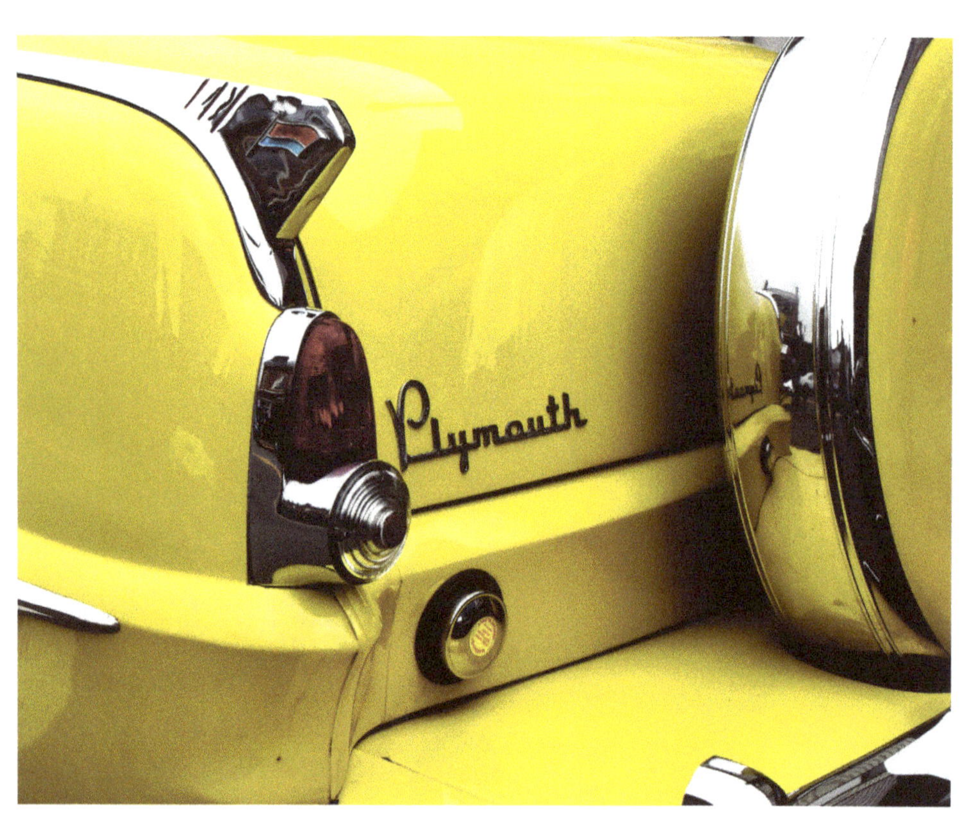
Plymouth

Where Do You Think You Are---1957?

After ordering a Seven and 7,
Salisbury steak, and
salad with 1,000 Island dressing,
the waiter asked:
*Where do you think you are---1957?*

Elvis shaking his tail,
Little Richard screaming, "I AM Tutti Frutti"
at White Bucks poseur Pat Boone,
Ike smiling calm and steady,
Ginsberg Howling,
Rosa resisting,
Little Rock 9 integrating,
ducks tailing, bees hiving,
juke boxes kicking.
Sputnik beeping,
French bikinis teasing,
Hemingway hunting in the African sun,
Kerouc searching without a map,
Atlas shrugging,
Miles and Monk improvising
in smoky dim lit haze,
Marilyn smiling that diamond gleam,
televisions glowing
before Bird's Eye dinners,

boundaries shifting,
coffee houses whispering
for poets to come with
rebellion in every napkin-written verse,
teenagers ignoring Cold War fears,
smoking Newports and
drinking warm Schlitz
at drive-in movies,
where romantic trysts unfolded.
Year of change.
Cultural spark.
Atomic Age legacy of
drifting souls with conflicted hearts
and coffee-stained fractured dreams

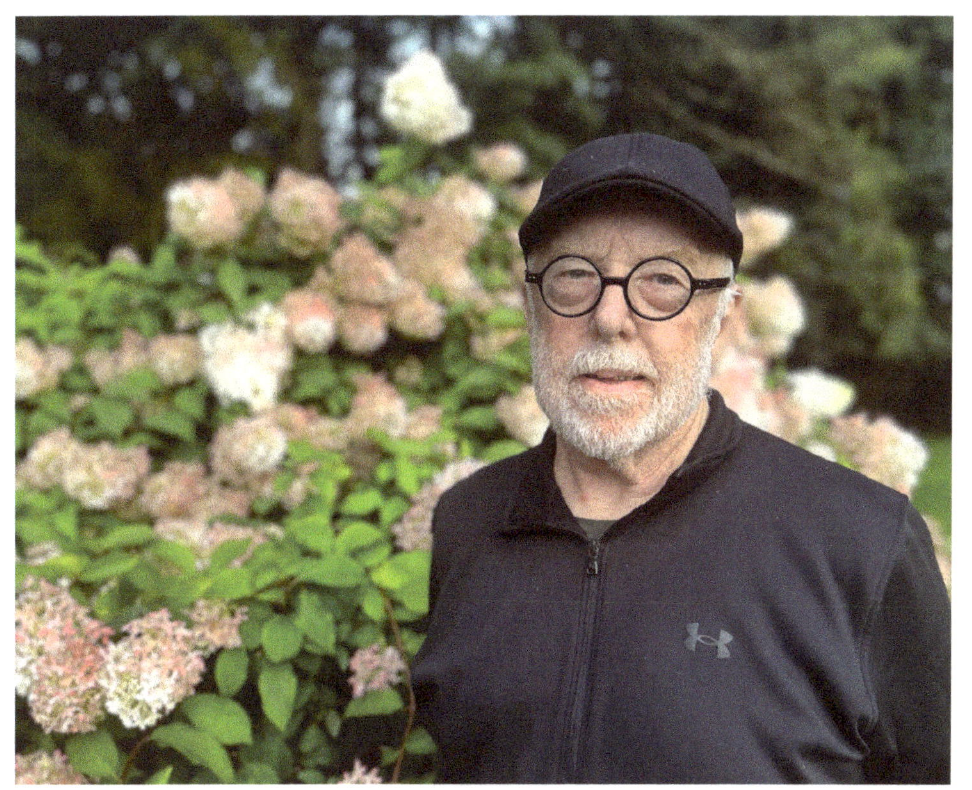

# ABOUT THE AUTHOR

Greg Clary was born and raised in Turkey Creek, West Virginia, and now resides in the northwestern Pennsylvania Wilds. He earned his Bachelor's and Master's degrees from Marshall University, his Ph.D. from Kent State University, and is Clarion University Professor Emeritus of Rehabilitation and Human Services.

His photographs have appeared in many publications including *The Sun Magazine, Looking at Appalachia, Rattle, Hole in the Head Review, Pine Mt Sand & Gravel, Tiny Seed Journal, The Watershed Journal, About Place, Change Seven, Appalachian Lit, Bee House Review, Fourth River,* and many more.

His writing and poetry have been published in *Rye Whiskey Review, The Bridge, Pine Mt. Sand & Gravel, Northern Appalachia Review, Pittsburgh Post-Gazette, Waccamaw Journal, Anti-Heroin Chic, Trailer Park Quarterly, Rust Belt Review, Clinch, Black Shamrock Magazine, Tobeco.* and *Wild Wind: Poems and Songs Inspired by the Songs of Robert Earl Keen.*

He is co-author of the ekphrastic photography/poetry book, *Piercing the Veil: Appalachian Visions (2020).*

www.ingramcontent.com/pod-product-compliance
Lightning Source LLC
Chambersburg PA
CBHW040805120726

48005CB00012B/1314